Mastering Interpersonal Skills

Mastering Personal and Interpersonal Skills

Peter F Haddon

Thorogood Publishing Ltd
10-12 Rivington Street
London EC2A 3DU
Telephone: 020 7749 4748
Fax: 020 7729 6110
Email: info@thorogoodpublishing.co.uk
Web: www.thorogoodpublishing.co.uk

A catalogue record for this book is available from the British Library

ISBN 1 85418 106 8

ISBN 1 85418 068 1 (Trade edition)

Printed in Great Britain by Ashford Colour Press

Published in South Africa as *Be The Best You Can* by Delta Books,
a division of Jonathan Ball Publishers (Pty) Ltd.

Acknowledgements

In writing this book I have been enormously influenced by and drawn insights and ideas from the books, audio and video tapes, lectures and seminars of many notable authorities in the field of personal development. I have attempted to bring together the principles and techniques which I have found to be most effective, not only in my life but in the lives of others whom I have had the privilege of influencing.

My knowledge and understanding of the development of human potential has been greatly affected by the following experts in their fields:

Richard Bandler	Jinny Ditzler	Jim Rohn
Og Mandino	Dr Stephen Covey	Tom Hopkins
Dr Reg Barrett	Dr Norman Vincent Peale	W Clement Stone
Dr Maxwell Maltz	Dr Wayne Dyer	Al Koran
Dr Kenneth Blanchard	Dr George Winslow Plummer	Paul G Thomas
Paul J Meyer	Dr Milton Erickson	Alan Lakein
Claude Bristol	Anthony Robbins	Brian Tracy
Dr Joseph Murphy	John Grinder	Dan Sullivan
Tony Buzan	Dr Robert Schuller	Caroline Leaf
Earl Nightingale	Dr Napoleon Hill	Dr Dennis Waitley
George S Clason	Dr David Schwartz	Dr H Spencer Lewis
John O'Keeffe		Zig Ziglar

I trust this book, inspired by these specialists, will serve to further advance the practical application of the philosophy to which they all subscribe: 'The seeds of future achievement are the thoughts of the present. If you will control your thoughts, you will control your destiny.'

Additionally, I am deeply grateful to the participants who have attended my personal development programmes and seminars over the years. My insight into human behaviour and motivation has been significantly enhanced by their contributions, both during the courses and in subsequent feedback.

Peter F Haddon

The author

Peter F Haddon

Peter F Haddon is the Managing Director of Top Achievers Limited, a London company specialising in 'helping the best get better.' He holds a B.Comm. and an MBA degree and is a qualified clinical hypnotherapist. He was formerly a Wing Commander in the then Rhodesian Air Force.

On the sports front, he captained Rhodesia at soccer on 11 occasions, including the 1970 World Cup. He also represented the Rhodesian Combined Services at boxing, soccer and water polo. He has written numerous articles and a best selling book on personal development. He has been involved in personal success coaching with sportsmen such as Francois Pienaar, the Captain of South Africa's 1995 World Cup winning rugby team; Mark McNulty, the international golfer; and Bruce Fordyce, the world's greatest ultra marathon runner.

Peter is acknowledged internationally as an outstanding speaker, trainer and personal success coach. He has developed a unique 'one to one' personal success coaching programme that has dramatically improved the performance and rewards of many successful entrepreneurs, sportsmen and women around the world.

Contents

Icons 6

Introduction 7

Chapter 1: **Using your true potential** 13

Left and right brain congruency 14

Right versus left brain 15

Desire 16

Habits..17

Mind maps 18

Autogenic conditioning 20

Imagination and willpower 23

Your subconscious mind 24

Summary..25

Activity 1: Autogenic conditioning 27

Chapter 2: **How to set your goals in life** 31

The subconscious mind 32

Values..37

'Why am I here?' 38

'Where am I?' 40

'Where do I want to be?'...41

Goal setting procedure 42

Rules for goal setting 42

Changing goals..49

Pain and pleasure associations 50

Summary..52

Activity 2: Identifying your values 55

Activity 3: Establishing your purpose in life 61

Activity 4: Where am I now? 62

Chapter 5: How to improve your self-image and self-confidence

Chapter 6: Self-motivation

Icons

Throughout the Masters in Management series of books you will see references and symbols in the margins. These are designed for ease of use and quick reference directing you quickly to key features of the text. The symbols used are:

	Key Question		Guide to Best Practice
	Action Checklist		Key Learning Point
	Activity		Key Management Concept

We would encourage you to use this book as a workbook, writing notes and comments in the margin as they occur. In this way we hope that you will benefit from the practical guidance and advice which this book provides.

There are exercises throughout this book. For your own convenience, we suggest that you use the sheets provided as a template, reproducing them as required according to the instruction given.

Introduction

Introduction

Over the years that I have been involved in personal development training, one question has consistently cropped up: 'Why is it that the results of motivational talks, tapes, videos, books, courses and seminars are limited and not long lasting?' I discovered that for motivational training to be truly effective, it was not enough to tell people what to do and how to do it. There are literally millions of people who know what to do and how to do it, but still do not go into action. The reason is that they have not re-programmed themselves for success. Naturally, they want to consistently produce positive results in their lives, yet they continue to follow their previously programmed limiting behavioural patterns. This is perfectly natural. We are creatures of habit and will tend to do tomorrow what we did yesterday and today. If we want different and more positive results, then we must behave differently and more positively than before. This requires a fundamental change in our thinking leading to changes in beliefs, attitudes, feelings and ultimately – behaviour. When the new behaviour is rewarded with the results we seek, we are far more likely to continue with it until it becomes a habit.

Most people use less than ten per cent of their true potential

Key Learning Point

Opinions vary as to the exact amount of our true potential that we actually use. However, there is general agreement that by and large most of us use no more than around ten per cent – at most. That is a pretty staggering statistic and a sad indictment of the human race. Stop and think about it for a moment. You are where you are today having used, at most, one tenth of your abilities. Just imagine what you could achieve and where you could be if you were aware of and knew how to use the other 90 per cent of untapped potential. The objective of this book is to help you recognise and use your full potential. It is practically orientated – designed to get you to **DO** certain things, many in fact, on a step-by-step basis. There are a number of activities provided for this purpose. Simply reading this book will not change anything in your life. If you are serious about making the most of your abilities, you will have to take action and the activities provided will enable you to practically apply the principles and techniques covered and thereby achieve meaningful results.

Francis Bacon was credited with the saying: 'Knowledge is power'. I believe he should have added two more words to make that statement completely true: 'Knowledge is power, when applied'. There is a multitude of people who have the knowledge and seem to delight in a lifetime pursuit of acquiring as much of it as possible. Yet they do absolutely nothing with it! This is fine for the few who have, as one of their goals, the desire to become accumulators of information. But, for the majority who sought the knowledge in the first place to put it to some use, it becomes increasingly frustrating. Think about the people you know. I'm sure you can immediately bring to mind someone who falls into this category.

Knowledge is power – when applied

Key Learning Point

I have a message for you. Don't waste your time reading this book if you lack the commitment to follow through and apply the knowledge you are about to learn. It is not intended for passive entertainment but for your active participation. It contains no magical formulae to transform you into an overnight success. There are no 'get rich quick' schemes. Instead you will find proven principles and laws of success which will enable you to become the winner you wish to be – *if you apply them.* They cannot work for you without you.

What does personal success mean to you? To some it conjures up ideas of wealth and materialistic possessions; to others happiness and fulfillment in their lives. But to many, perhaps the majority, it is a measure of how they rate against their colleagues. This is wrong. You will never be truly successful by constantly comparing your performance with others. At best you will only become a second rate version of who and what they are. Rather, your yardstick of success should be your own potential performance. The definition of success that I prefer is: 'Success is the progressive realisation of your genuinely desired goals.' If you adopt this definition as your own then you will start to look upon success as a journey rather than a destination and will set your own standards of performance to measure your progress along the way.

Your goal should be progress – not perfection

Key Learning Point

The most important investment you will ever make is in your own development. The price that you have paid for this book is a mere drop in the ocean to the return that it will bring you, provided you are serious about making the most of your life and are consequently prepared to take the time and effort to do what is asked of you.

What you do with your life is your responsibility – no one else's. Of course you can find so-called 'reasons' for not being successful, such as your lack of education or experience, insufficient money, your upbringing, social class, race, religion and so on. These are not reasons – they're excuses. It is easy to blame other people, circumstances beyond your control, the government, the economy, the weather or whatever else comes to mind for your situation in life. But it is an act of self delusion. If you are one of those who points fingers – stop right now. Otherwise, your commitment will be lacking because you will have a ready made 'cop-out'. Decide right now that the only one responsible for your success in life is – *you*.

The only one responsible for your success in life is you

A word of warning before you begin. It is an unfortunate fact that less than ten per cent of readers of non-fiction books such as this one, ever read beyond the first chapter. So before you even start, make a commitment to yourself right now that you will not just read the book from cover to cover but will practically apply its contents. As a measure of this commitment, diarise to spend at least one hour per day on this book. Please do not read this book once and put it back on your bookshelf with the intention of coming back to it at some later stage to undertake the activities. *That does not work.* Your decision to carry out the activities should be made before you read the book the first time. Your destiny is shaped by the decisions you take in life. Make a committed decision today to take charge of your life by following through on this book. Decide to become one of the few who do, rather than one of the many who talk. Realise that a single reading and then a place on your bookshelf to gather dust will not change anything in your life. You need to read, re-read, study, assimilate and apply its contents. It should be your constant companion, within reach most of the time. I suggest you initially read it through from cover to cover without attempting any of the activities or exercises. These should be carried out on the second and subsequent readings. These activities will create an awareness of exactly who you are, what you want from life and how you are going to get it.

Successful people have something in common. They have a system which works for them. This book will provide you with an effective means of attaining success as it is all about change, development, achievement and fulfillment.

Using your true potential

. . . .

Chapter 1

Left and right brain congruency

The key to using your true potential and mastering personal and interpersonal skills lies in obtaining left and right brain congruency. Your left brain is the logical, analytical, verbal, sequential, statistical hemisphere whereas your right brain is the creative, artistic, imaginative, spacial, holistic, rhythmic, colour and dimension orientated hemisphere. That is a pretty long winded description. In simple terms the left hemisphere is dominant in controlling willpower and discipline whilst the right hemisphere is dominant in controlling imagination and emotion. If you are a product of the westernised education system, there is a good chance that you are predominantly left brain orientated and have been largely unaware of the tremendous right brain power that you possess. It is analogous to having two powerful outboard motors on a motorboat and only using one of them. Yet, where your brain is concerned, it results in far less than a 50 per cent utilisation of the power available. The engines are designed to work in tandem and are complementary to each other. Exactly the same applies with your left and right brain hemispheres. Most goal setting exercises of any value will encourage you to write out affirmation cards and repeat the goal statements to yourself on an ongoing basis. This is left brain activity. You will certainly attain far more success in your life by repeating affirmations than you would without them. However, it is like using just the one outboard motor. If you are repeating positive statements to yourself on an ongoing basis but simultaneously, your right brain is conjuring up pictures that contradict those affirmations, you have a recipe for frustration. You will go much further by combining left and right brain activity and following the autogenic conditioning process outlined in this book which ensures left and right brain congruency. Other means of obtaining left and right brain co-operation are the regular use of mind maps and goals posters. These will be discussed in detail later in this chapter and in Chapter 3.

The left hemisphere is dominant in controlling willpower and discipline whilst the right hemisphere is dominant in controlling imagination and emotion

Right versus left brain

Have you ever participated in a weight loss programme? You may well have found like so many others that the diet that you embarked upon, coupled with an exercise regimen, worked for you and indeed you did lose your weight. You may have even attained your new goal weight. But did it last? If you are honest, the answer is probably NO. Statistics in the United States of America indicate that most people who embark on a weight loss programme tend to weigh approximately one kilogram (2.2 pounds) more than they did when they started the programme two years previously! Now that is not to suggest that the diets and exercise programmes do not work. Most of them do. However, it is the power of your mind that comes into the picture. Where your weight loss programme is being governed by only the left brain, with your right brain being allowed to imagine and emotionalise things to eat or do which do not support your diet and worse still, if your right brain is associating pain with the action steps that you are taking to lose that weight, sooner or later the right brain will overpower the left brain and you will revert to your previous habits. The danger then is that you may never again embark on a plan to achieve your goals because you do not believe you have the capability. Now this same tendency applies in the pursuit of whatever other goals we may have set for ourselves in our lives. So the key to achieving consistent results in our lives is to get our right and left brains working together for the common goal. This pre-supposes that effective personal development training must include exercises and activities which are related to the development of the right brain as well as interaction between both the right and left brains so as to achieve the desired congruency and progressively build new goal directed behavioural habits.

Key Learning Point

The key to achieving consistent results in our lives is to get our right and left brains working together for the common goal

Desire

When discussing the qualities that enable people to become highly successful, the list would probably include perseverance, drive, determination, discipline, self-confidence, initiative and the like. However, there is one overriding characteristic of successful people which, if not present, would not give rise to these other qualities. This is *desire*. You will never go higher than the genuine desires that you hold. This means that when setting goals and developing plans to attain them you need to have very strong, compelling reasons for these goals. If the desire is not strong enough, sooner or later you will find ways to sabotage your own action steps. You need to be in a position to regularly fuel this desire. This entails constantly reminding yourself of the successes that you are having on a daily basis and being able to visualise and emotionalise the end result of your goals – the rewards and benefits that will accrue to you and your loved ones on successful attainment. There is a process for doing just this. It involves right brain activity (no surprise!) and takes a certain amount of time each day, (I recommend a total of 40 minutes), to mentally rehearse your goals and plans of action. When you are regularly fuelling your own fire of desire every day (right brain), you will have the level of motivation needed to follow the steps that you have planned to take (left brain) to achieve your goals.

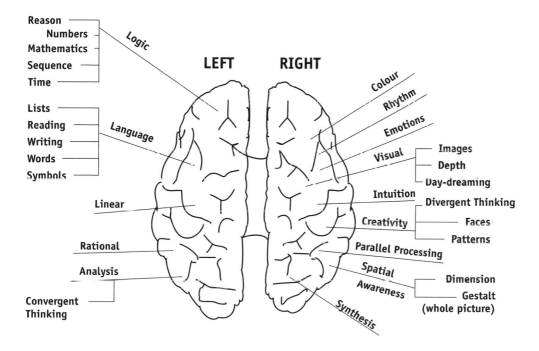

Figure 1: Specialisations of the left and right brain

For your life to change – you must change

Key Learning Point

Habits

For the circumstances in your life to change, YOU must change. No personal development book, cassette tape, video, training programme or seminar will ensure your desired success unless it facilitates the acquisition of new behavioural habits and when provision is made to reinforce and support these habits after acquisition. This unfortunately is where the seminars of short duration fall down. Now don't get me wrong. I am not knocking the shorter seminars. In fact we often run them ourselves. However, we must be absolutely clear about the objectives of these seminars. If long-term results are to be achieved, then habits have to be changed and generally speaking, it takes between 21 and 30 days to acquire a new habit. It is therefore, completely unrealistic to expect long-term results from short-term seminars/workshops/courses or by merely reading a book. When course participants are given activities to carry out both on an individual and a group basis and consequently apply the principles and techniques which they learn on the programme into their own lives and see the results of those applications, their new-found behaviour is being reinforced and rewarded leading to the development of the right habits. However, habits once acquired need to be sustained and this requires follow-up mechanisms to be in place. Hence, any effective personal development programme which guarantees measurable results must provide not only for the acquisition of new habits but also sufficient follow-up to sustain them. An accountability process needs to be set up to regularly monitor activity level and results.

Key Management Concept

Mind maps

If our right brains are that crucial to our personal success, what techniques can we use to exercise them regularly so that they operate in harmony with our left brain? The research conducted by Dr Roger Sperry and later enhanced by the work of Tony Buzan has indicated that one of the most powerful tools to obtaining left and right brain congruency is the consistent use of mind maps. Mind mapping is a technique whereby information is summarised in a form of pictorial representation which depends very much on the creativity of the individual involved. The idea is that when information is pictured in colourful word associations backed up by sketches or even stick drawings of the key words, it is far more easily remembered, much like when looking at a photograph you can recall in detail the happenings that led up to and followed the incident.

There are a few basic rules or guidelines to follow for effective mind mapping.

Basic rules for mind mapping

1. In the centre of the page have the core theme spelt out and with as much colour as possible. It should be portrayed within a central image.

2. Wherever possible use one word per line and ensure these words are printed. The length of the lines from the central image should be the same as the length of the word written on the line.

3. Use as much colour as your creativity demands.

4. Use images in addition to or even in place of words. Images will greatly improve your ability to recall information. Many people believe that they are not artistic and are therefore reluctant to put down on paper simple drawings of the word representations. This is nonsense. They have probably not been using their right brain for so many years that they are unaware of the creativity that they possess within them. Like anything else, their creativity will be developed once they start practicing.

5. Use codes for abbreviations. These codes must have meaning for you – not necessarily someone else. However standard symbols such as: = (equals); > (greater than); < (less than); ↑ (increase); ↓ (decrease) + (more); – (less) and the like, should be used where relevant.

6. Associate different parts of your mind map, where necessary, by the use of arrows. Where you wish to connect one portion of your mind map with more than one other, use a multi-headed arrow with different colours and different thicknesses of lines to represent the importance of the associations to you.

Guide to Best Practice

Whilst I have referred to these as mind mapping rules, they should not be construed as hard and fast laws. An effective mind map is one that works for you and therefore it is your tailoring and your emphasis, images, colours, codes and style that will determine its effectiveness. Try to develop the habit of taking down all your notes in mind map format. If you are required to give presentations, do this from a mind map. When you are at meetings, take down the minutes in mind map layout and just notice the difference in your ability to retain exactly what happened at that meeting and compare it with your usual logical/analytical method of recording minutes.

If you would like more in-depth knowledge of mind mapping I would recommend: *The Mind Map Book: Radiant Thinking* by Tony Buzan and Barry Buzan published by BBC Books, a division of BBC Enterprises Limited, Woodlands, Wood Lane, London, W12 0TT.

Autogenic conditioning

A tremendously powerful technique for obtaining left and right brain congruency is autogenic conditioning. This was the name given to the very simple process, which I will shortly explain, by Professor Johannes Schultz in the 1920s. However, it was only in the 1980s that we in the western world started sitting up and taking notice of the power of this technique when we analysed the reasons why the East Germans and Russians were winning all the gold medals at the Olympic Games. We initially thought it might be their physical training techniques but this proved not to be the case. In fact, if anything, their physical training methods were outdated compared to those being used in the western world. The big difference in the athletes' preparation was that they embarked on autogenic conditioning, a form of mental rehearsal or preview of the event they were physically preparing for. The results of using autogenic conditioning techniques in the sports field are now widely known and accepted. Yet, surprisingly, these same techniques have not been employed by people in their everyday lives to maximise their own potential. Let's be perfectly clear about what autogenic conditioning can and cannot do. It certainly cannot turn an average athlete into an Olympic champion overnight. However, what it can do is enable that athlete to perform at his or her best when they choose, for example, in the key moments of a competition.

I have personally utilised autogenic conditioning in my own life and it forms a fundamental part of my personal development and coaching programmes which have been running for the last 17 years. I am absolutely convinced that it is the most effective technique for fuelling your desire level on an ongoing basis and thereby ensuring that you are maximising your potential – *if it is regularly used*. Like so many other principles and techniques, it is one thing knowing it and another thing entirely applying it.

There are four stages to autogenic conditioning; progressive relaxation, verbalisation, visualisation and emotionalisation.

a) **Progressive relaxation**

Guide to Best Practice

- Seat yourself in an armchair with your buttocks as far back in the chair as you can and your spine pressing against the chair back. Have your feet uncrossed and placed flat on the floor. Your hands should rest in your lap. When commencing the relaxation phase, a useful 'trigger' to obtaining the relaxed state is to make a circle with your thumb and forefinger. Do this with both hands. When you have completed your autogenic conditioning session (ie. 20 minutes later), and you are visualising your body becoming re-energised, utilise the other re-energising 'trigger' of making a circle with your thumb and middle finger. Again, do this with both hands. In a short while these 'triggers' will become synonymous with your relaxed and energised states and you will be able to access these states simply by activating the relevant triggers. (I have given you certain suggestions to assist your body to progressively relax in Activity No 1 at the end of this chapter.)

b) Verbalisation

- In this stage you initially read the affirmations on your 3" x 5" cards which you will have compiled after having completed the goal setting activities in Chapter 2. After a while, once these affirmations have been committed to memory, you need no longer use this stage but proceed directly to the next stage – visualisation.

c) Visualisation

- You now project a picture of the desired end result onto an imaginary screen in front of you. You see yourself with your goals fulfilled and enjoying the rewards and benefits that will flow from them. This takes the form of a dissociated picture where you are seeing yourself on the screen separated from the actual experience, rather like watching a movie with you playing the leading role.

d) Emotionalisation

- This differs from the previous stage in that you now mentally transport yourself into the picture on the screen becoming fully associated with it and experience with as many senses as you can, all the emotions attached to the successful accomplishment of your goal.

Imagination and willpower

Why is our right brain so powerful? To answer this let's have a brief look at the results of Dr Emile Coué who in the early 1900s was achieving a far greater recovery rate with his patients than were his fellow medical doctors. Naturally they wanted to know what he was doing that they were not. Surprisingly, they found that he was prescribing the same medications as they were to treat diagnosed illnesses. However, they also found that he encouraged his patients, as part of their treatment, to look in the mirror first thing in the morning and last thing at night and say to themselves in a convincing manner: 'Each day, in every way, I'm getting better and better.' This statement when repeated over and over again with conviction gradually became a belief and their minds simply instructed their bodies to conform with the belief. Emile Coué subsequently formulated Coué's Law which states that: 'Whenever imagination and willpower are in conflict, imagination will inevitably win.' In other words, if we have left and right brain conflict and are attempting to achieve our goals by means of willpower alone, there is a very good chance that we will sabotage our own actions unless and until we ensure that our right brain, our imagination and emotional mechanism, is working with and not against left brain willpower and discipline. One of the major functions of your brain is to sustain life and protect you from what it perceives to be pain. Consequently, whilst you may have tremendous willpower and discipline, this will never be enough if your right brain imagines the short-term pain that might result by virtue of taking the action steps that you are contemplating. The trick here is to use autogenic conditioning regularly so that you bring to bear the fantastic power of the right brain onto your goals and use your imagination and emotion to focus on the long-term pleasure that will result from taking the action steps contemplated. You can also use your imagination to focus on the much greater long-term pain that will result from **NOT** taking the action steps. Your brain will always do more to avoid pain than to gain pleasure. More will be said about this principle in subsequent chapters.

Key Learning Point

Emile Coué's Law

'Whenever imagination and willpower are in conflict, imagination will inevitably win'

Your success in life will come about by virtue of your performance – not your potential. You may well have all the potential that you will ever need to succeed but that is by no means a guarantee of your success. The only way that you will ensure success is by maximising your potential through your actions. As your behaviour is determined by your attitude and feelings, it is imperative that you maintain your desire and therefore, your motivation at a high level if you are to behave in accordance with your capabilities. This is achieved by daily autogenic conditioning.

Your subconscious mind

I will be discussing the subconscious mind further in Chapter 2: 'How to set your goals in life' but at this stage, you may well be wondering where the subconscious and conscious functions of the mind fit in with left and right brain hemispheres. Is the subconscious mind predominantly a function of one or other of these hemispheres? The activity of your brain is measured by the amount of electrical energy generated. You have at any one time different brainwave frequencies. Whilst you are reading this, your brain is operating mainly at the beta level which is between 13 and 30 cycles per second. When you embark upon your autogenic conditioning exercises, you enter the alpha level which is that pleasant drowsy state that you are in just before dropping off to sleep at night or first thing in the morning when you awaken. Your brainwave frequency in the alpha level is between eight and 13 cycles per second. This is the state where your subconscious mind is most readily accessed. Your subconscious is no longer being dominated by the conscious mind from a filtration of information point of view. There are two further levels of brainwave frequency namely theta – between four and eight cycles per second and delta – less than four cycles per second. Theta is generally representative of sleep and delta of either a very deep sleep or a state of unconsciousness. (You may well know certain people who appear to be in delta for much of their waking life!)

If you understand how important the alpha state is to programme your subconscious mind with the positive beliefs and instructions of your choice, you may correctly conclude that the subconscious mind is largely a right brain function. The research of Dr Roger Sperry, mentioned earlier, suggests that should the corpus callosum (the joint between the two brain hemispheres) be severed for any reason or the right brain become inoperable, the left brain would then take over the functions of the right brain and consequently the subconscious functioning would then become a left brain activity. However, for our purposes, assuming both sides of our brain are operating normally, the subconscious process can be perceived as being predominantly a right brain activity.

Summary

Key Learning Point

1. The key to personal success lies in obtaining left and right brain congruency.

2. The left brain is instrumental in controlling willpower and discipline. The right brain controls imagination and emotion.

3. Techniques to obtain left and right brain congruency include autogenic conditioning, the regular use of mind maps and the construction of a goals poster.

4. Desire is the common denominator of personal success qualities. Daily use of autogenic conditioning will ensure that your desire remains at a high level and in turn leads to results-orientated behaviour.

5. The acquisition of supporting behavioural habits is a pre-requisite to consistently achieving the results you desire. Any habit takes on average between 21 and 30 days to cultivate.

6. One habit to develop is the regular use of mind mapping. Following the basic rules or guidelines, use mind mapping for taking notes, minutes of meetings, presentations, records of daily happenings and the like.

7. The most effective tool you can use for your own personal success is autogenic conditioning. By carrying out 20 minutes of autogenic conditioning twice a day, you will be programming yourself for personal success. The four stages of autogenic conditioning are:

    a) Progressive relaxation

    b) Verbalisation

    c) Visualisation

    d) Emotionalisation

8. The right brain is far more powerful than the left brain. Remember Emile Coué's Law: 'Whenever imagination and willpower are in conflict, imagination will inevitably win.' The key to obtaining right and left brain congruency is therefore using your imagination for you in conjunction with your willpower, rather than allowing it to be used against you.

9. Your success in life will come about by virtue of your performance – not your potential. Results stem from action – not talk!

10. Your subconscious – your success mechanism – is largely a right brain function. To maximise its power, you need to constantly exercise your right brain.

Key Learning Points

If this is your first reading, please proceed to Chapter 2. If this is your second or subsequent reading, please carry out Activity No. 1.

Activity No.1

Activity

Autogenic conditioning

This procedure should be carried out for 20 minutes, twice a day (ideally first thing in the morning immediately after you wake up and again in the evening just before you retire for the night).

The four stages of autogenic conditioning are:

a) Progressive relaxation

c) Visualisation

b) Verbalisation

d) Emotionalisation

(These stages have been briefly described in this chapter, pages 21 and 22).

Progressive relaxation

This is achieved by sitting in a chair with your feet flat on the floor and your hands lightly clasped in your lap. You should loosen any items of tight clothing which might make you feel uncomfortable. Close your eyes and start focusing your attention on your feet. Concentrate on feeling your toes and feet relaxing completely. Wriggle your toes slightly to be more aware of them and then allow them to relax. Your feet now feel completely relaxed. Relaxation now spreads over your insteps, around your ankles and into the calves of your legs. Focus your attention on your calves and allow them to relax. Flex your calf muscles slightly to be more aware of them and then allow them to relax. Your calf muscles are now feeling completely relaxed and relaxation continues over your knees and into your thigh muscles. Tense your thigh muscles to be more aware of them and then allow them to relax completely. You can feel them becoming more relaxed. Your thighs are now completely relaxed. Both of your legs are now so relaxed that they feel limp and heavy. Imagine relaxation spreading now around your hips and your abdomen like a blanket. You are concentrating on that particular area of your body and you can feel all the muscles around your stomach relaxing. Your stomach now feels extremely relaxed. All the muscles around your rib cage, midriff and diaphragm are now fully relaxed. You are now becoming aware that your breathing is deeper than usual. Concentrate on your breathing for a few seconds. Breathe deeply and rhythmically and feel your body relaxing as your breaths become deeper. Relaxation now spreads around your back muscles and, as you allow them to relax they blend into the chair in which you are sitting and you feel extremely comfortable and content sitting in that position. Relaxation continues up your spine, through your nervous system relaxing muscle, tissues and sinew all over your body. You can now feel the relaxation spreading over and under your shoulder blades and you allow them to relax completely. As you relax your shoulders completely you allow them to droop into a more comfortable position. You now feel relaxation spreading down both of your upper arms and spreading across your elbows into your forearms and across your wrists and into your hands. You can now feel the relaxation spreading into the tips of your fingers and you feel a slight tingling sensation as the relaxation reaches them. You now allow the muscles around your neck and throat to relax and your head begins to feel a little heavy. You permit it to droop towards your chest. Relaxation now spreads into all of your facial muscles, and the frown lines around your eyes and across your forehead are now smoothed out. The smallest muscles in your body, those in your eyelids, are now relaxed and your eyelids feel very heavy. Your whole body now feels totally relaxed. You feel yourself slipping gently into a deeper and deeper state of complete and utter relaxation. Your breathing is now deep and rhythmic and with each deep rhythmic breath you become more and more pleasantly relaxed. Any background noises that you hear serve only to induce a deeper state of relaxation.

You should use the above suggestions to talk yourself down into this deep level of relaxation every time you embark on your autogenic conditioning exercise until you have spent two weeks continuously performing this exercise twice daily. At that stage, you will not need to talk yourself down into a deep state of relaxation but merely visualise yourself in this position and within seconds you will be in that deep state. To accelerate the depth of relaxation, it is advisable to have soft background music played at a one-beat-per-second rhythm as this induces the right mood and environment for a deeply relaxed state.

Verbalisation

In this deep level of relaxation, verbalise the statements of your major goals using the goal affirmation cards compiled in Activity 8. Repeat each goal statement six times before verbalising the next one. Confine these affirmations to a maximum of four goals. Once a goal has been achieved the affirmation card relating to that goal must be replaced by another.

Visualisation

Close your eyes and picture an imaginary screen in front of you. Project onto that screen clear, colourful, detailed pictures of yourself with your four major goals achieved. See yourself and your loved ones enjoying the rewards and benefits of the successful attainment of those goals. Carry out this process for each one of your four major goals separately.

Initially, you may find it extremely difficult to focus your mind on a particular goal for more than a minute or so. This is perfectly natural if you have never before engaged in any form of meditation, yoga, alpha training or other creative visualisation techniques. Don't worry. With daily practice your concentration ability will progressively improve and within 30 days you should be able to focus your mind on your chosen goal for as long as you wish. It is important when commencing this exercise not to force yourself to concentrate when you find your mind wandering, as, otherwise, you will develop a headache. Rather, gently bring your mind back and think about different aspects of the goal to those you initially focused upon. In fact, for the first three days, allow yourself to experience the benefits of the alpha state such as the deep level of complete physical relaxation, the settling and clarification of your thoughts and the re-vitalised feeling at the end of each 20 minute session. On the fourth day begin to direct your mind onto your four major goals, one at a time.

There are two areas of focus when carrying out this creative visualisation exercise. Initially, the focus should be on the end result. Once you can readily bring to mind crystal clear pictures of the end result (ie. enjoying the fruits of successful goal attainment), you can then switch your focus onto the process – the action plan which you intend to follow to achieve your goal. In this manner you will quickly start to generate ideas on how best to change your existing plan, if necessary, based on the daily feed back of the results of your current actions.

Emotionalisation

In this stage you mentally transport yourself into the pictures you have been visualising and experience the feelings as intensely as you can using all of your senses. You are now fully associated with the picture, no longer seeing yourself from a detached, passive standpoint, but actively experiencing the sensations that your successes have produced.

Re-energising

At the end of the 20 minute session, talk yourself up (to the beta brainwave level) over 20 seconds by suggesting to yourself the following: 'Take a deep breath – in through the nose and out through the mouth. Feel the energy returning to the body as it gradually replaces the relaxation. I am going to count backwards from 20 to 0 and as I count up I will progressively feel more and more energised until I reach 0 when I will open my eyes and feel completely re-vitalised.'

After two weeks the 20 second count up can be reduced to 10 seconds and after a further four weeks five seconds. After about three months you will be able to enter and leave alpha at will.

How to set your goals in life

Chapter 2

George Bernard Shaw once said: 'Anyone who doesn't know what he wants in life will have to be satisfied with what he gets.' That statement is as true today as it was then. You can't get what you want unless you know what you want. And, strange as it may seem, most people do not know what they want. They may think that they do but these usually turn out to be vague notions of dreamy utopian situations which, deep down, they know will never materialise. They have never sat down and written out exactly what they will be, do or have in the future or, if they ever did attempt such an exercise, it probably resulted in fuzzy generalisations rather than detailed specifics.

If you can't get what you want until you know what you want, how do you make sure that you know what you want? Effective goal setting is the answer. This is the starting point of all meaningful achievement. Fortunately, being goal directed is a natural characteristic of human beings. In fact, goal attainment is how we individuals become fulfilled and happy and businesses achieve success in the market place. The trick, both in private and business life, is knowing how to use goal setting effectively. That is the objective of this chapter.

The subconscious mind

In Chapter 1, I mentioned that the operation of the subconscious mind was mainly a right brain function. I feel it necessary at this stage to explain its function in a little more detail so that you will understand how it fits in with the goal setting process. I do not intend neither here nor anywhere else in this book to enter into any in-depth discussions on the composition and biological functioning of the conscious and subconscious minds, as there is even disagreement amongst medical practitioners as to whether we possess a separate conscious and subconscious mind or a single mind with two separate functions. Be that as it may, there is agreement on the fact that the subconscious mind (or function) is irrational, illogical and accepts as facts any suggestions continuously fed to it. The subconscious mind will not question whatever orders or instructions are given to it by the conscious mind but will carry them out slavishly whether they are positive or negative.

In the same way that you do not have to be a qualified electrician to use electrical appliances or an automobile engineer to drive your car, you do not need to have specialist knowledge on the biological functioning of your subconscious mind in order to use its tremendous power. You can liken it to a computer which needs to be programmed if it is to be effective. The programmer in this case is your conscious mind. The function of your subconscious mind is to transform the input you give it in the form of thoughts, ideas, suggestions, orders or instructions into reality. As with other computers, the output is only as good as the input. If you insert negative information in the form of thoughts of failure, apprehension or doubt then the output will be correspondingly negative. The opposite of course is also true. Positive input will produce positive results. Consequently, you must develop the habit of continuously seeing yourself and your achievements in a positive light. You need to constantly project onto the screen of your mind pictures of the successful attainment of your goals, with everyone concerned enjoying the benefits and rewards of your achievements.

The function of your subconscious mind is to transform the input you give it in the form of thoughts, ideas, suggestions, orders or instructions into reality

Key Learning Point

Let me use another analogy to further illustrate the functioning of the subconscious mind. It is similar to a plot of fertile soil which facilitates the cultivation and growth of whatever seeds are sown. You've heard the old adage: 'You reap what you sow.' Your conscious mind is the gardener, responsible for sowing the right seeds in the garden – your subconscious mind. It would be ludicrous to plant say bean seeds and then expect potatoes to grow from them.

Yet that is what so many people are doing on a regular basis. They are sowing seeds of negativity but expecting positive results to grow from them. It simply cannot happen. You can only realistically expect positive results in your life when you consistently sow positive seeds – visualisations and emotionalisations of the end results that you desire. You will then be causing your subconscious mind to act – to attract to you the ideas, people or circumstances which will enable your goals to be brought to fruition.

The output of your subconscious mind is in the form of habits. Every habit is acquired through conscious repetition of certain acts until they become subconsciously automatic. Again, to use the computer analogy, your habits in effect become programmes which are stored in your subconscious mind and retrieved and used at the discretion of the programmer, your conscious mind. A positive mental attitude is an acquired habit as is self-confidence, self-discipline, enthusiasm – in fact all qualities generally associated with successful people. These qualities can all be developed by the regular programming of your subconscious mind.

Key Learning Point

The subconscious mind cannot differentiate between a real and a vividly imagined experience

Let's assume that you are an introvert, shy and reserved never having attempted to be more assertive and outgoing because of one or more past negative experiences. You do not have to remain as you are unless you choose to do so. Instead, you can change your programme. The subconscious mind cannot differentiate between a real and a vividly imagined experience. This means that you can programme yourself with vividly imagined positive experiences which will have the same effect, as far as the conditioning process is concerned, as actual experiences. You can also replay past negative experiences in your mind but this time, of course, with a successful outcome. This is all part of your positive conditioning process. But a word of warning here. Because it seems so simple to just relax and visualise yourself as the successful person you are soon to become, displaying all of your positive qualities and enjoying the fruits of your achievements, do not underestimate the importance of the exercise. I have already explained the process of autogenic conditioning in Chapter 1 as the means to fuel your desire on an ongoing basis. If you adopt the habit of carrying out this exercise twice a day for 20 minutes you will be, perhaps for the first time since you were about seven years old, putting your imagination to work in a constructive, controlled and goal orientated manner.

The programmes which you produce are sets of stored information, instructions and orders. The programming process is automatic and is taking place continuously, either consciously or unconsciously. Therefore, to ensure that your programming is positive, you need to take charge of the process yourself and commence a regular schedule of affirmations, visualisations and emotionalisations covering the goals you seek. If you do not take charge of this programming process, you are, in effect, allowing your subconscious mind to be programmed haphazardly and involuntarily with predominantly negative suggestions from other 'followers'.

It is far more important who you become in reaching for your goals than the actual attainment of them

There are several important points to realise when taking deliberate control of the programming of your subconscious mind:

1. The role of the conscious mind is to habitually feed the sub-conscious mind with thoughts, in the form of crystal-clear images of your major goals already achieved.

2. The role of the sub-conscious mind is to transform these images into feelings and behaviours.

3. The sub-conscious mind is controlled by the power of suggestion. It accepts whatever suggestions are repeatedly imparted to it whether they are true or false.

4. The reasoning of the subconscious is deductive. It is incapable of inductive reasoning.

5. It tends to repeat previously learned behavioural patterns until they are replaced by new ones.

6. It cannot be programmed positively by using negative suggestions.

You cannot positively programme your subconscious mind by suggestions of what it must not do. For example, you should not use 'I don't want to fail' if you want to succeed, as your sub-conscious will focus on the word 'fail'. Instead you should feed it positive affirmations about the person you are to become, such as:

'I am successful, happy and prosperous.'

'I am a kind, loving person who cares about people.'

'I am growing every day by doing the best that I can in every situation.'

'I give better service every day by constantly asking myself how I can add more value to others.'

'I have the power of choice and I choose abundance, security, happiness and peace of mind.'

None of your goals stand any chance of being realised without your taking action. Your actions are determined by your feelings which are generated by your beliefs which are instilled by your own repeated thoughts and suggestions. Consequently, the seeds you are sowing in the form of the thoughts and suggestions you are implanting into your subconscious mind as images must manifest themselves in goal-directed behaviour. It cannot happen otherwise.

Values

The pursuit of your goals should never be at the expense of your deeply held values. Quite the opposite in fact. The actual process of attaining your goals should give expression to and reinforce those values. It is far more important who you become in reaching for your goals than the actual attainment of them. If you have to sacrifice or transgress some of your meaningful values (such as honesty, sincerity, humility, integrity, concern for others, feeling of contribution, happiness, contentment, kindness, empathy and so on) in order to 'succeed' in life, then sooner or later you will wake up to the fact that you are not being true to yourself and that your success is largely hollow and will never give you the feeling of fulfilment that you are seeking. You may well be 'successful' in the eyes of others if their judgement of you is based on the materialistic trappings of success. But you know how you attained them – and that is something you will have to live with for the rest of your life. To ensure that your goals help you to live in accordance with your values you need to establish a hierarchy of the most important ones and then identify your major purpose in life which will naturally embrace those values. Your goals are then set with your purpose and values as the foundations. It is an inter-active process. Your values determine your purpose and goals. The intensity of your desire for your goals determines your actions. In turn your actions lead to the reinforcement of your desire for, and the attainment of, your goals which give expression to your purpose and values.

The first steps toward making your life more successful entail answering four simple questions: 'Why Am I Here?', 'Where Am I?', 'Where Do I Want To Be?' and 'How Do I Get There?' The first three questions will be answered in this chapter and the fourth in Chapter 3 dealing with the planning process.

Figure 2: Taking action

'Why am I here?'

The answer to this question should identify an overriding purpose in your life.

The need for a purpose

During the second World War Dr. Viktor Frankl, one of the world's foremost psychiatrists, spent three years as a prisoner of war in four German concentration camps. In studying his fellow prisoners he found that their chances of survival depended more on their having a reason to live than on their physical condition. Those who could see a meaning – some purpose – to their suffering, survived. Dr. Frankl countered the camp's influence on the prisoners by counselling them, giving them inner strength by helping them to identify a purpose in their lives and goals which they could look forward to achieving in the future. The point I want to make here is that if it was so important for prisoners of war in a concentration camp to have a purpose in their lives, surely it is much more important for you who has, relatively speaking, the freedom of choice, to establish a purpose in your life. This is the essential prerequisite to effective goal setting.

For what would you most like to be remembered? If the answer immediately springs to mind, then you already have a clear cut purpose in your life. If, however, you have to think about the question for a while and then still not be too sure whether or not you have the right answer, your purpose has not been clearly defined. Assume that you wanted to be remembered for helping others. Just how do you see yourself doing that? Can you describe in specific detail how you plan to use your abilities, qualities and skills to assist others?

If you are in any doubt as to your main purpose in life then you need to spend some time clarifying it before commencing your goal setting exercise. Setting goals becomes so much more effective and meaningful once your purpose has been established, as the attainment of the goals leads to the fulfilment of that purpose. Many people commence goal setting without first having established their main purpose in life. They are successful – to a limited extent – but eventually reach the point where they no longer derive satisfaction from attaining their goals, precisely because they do not lead to the realisation of a single main purpose. Any goal setting exercise is better than none at all but to be truly effective it must aim at an overall purpose.

Your individual purpose in life can be likened to a country's constitution or a company's mission statement, both of which proclaim values, standards or principles under which goals are set. Your purpose should be your own statement of how you plan to live your life. It should form the basis of your decision making in all areas of your life and, as mentioned earlier, should embrace the values that are most important to you.

Your purpose should embrace your most important values and form the basis for your decision making in all areas of your life

Key Learning Point

Key Question

'Where am I?'

Suppose you are travelling through a town that is new to you, take a wrong turning and find that you're lost. You then consult your map and locate the destination you were seeking originally. Fine – but this is not enough – you must also know where you are right now. Only when you have those two points, where you are and where you want to go to, can you plot your route. It is the same with goal setting. You need to know where you are in life as well as where you want to be.

Resources

Determining just where you are entails an objective assessment of your personal resources – your traits or qualities; assets and liabilities; significant achievements; hobbies and interests; job likes and dislikes; influences arising from people, experiences, or events; family relationships and values.

'Where do I want to be?'

Key Question

Having identified your purpose and your resources, you are now ready to answer the third question, 'Where do I want to be?', by setting goals in the seven areas of your life: *physical, mental, social, spiritual, personal, business* and *financial*.

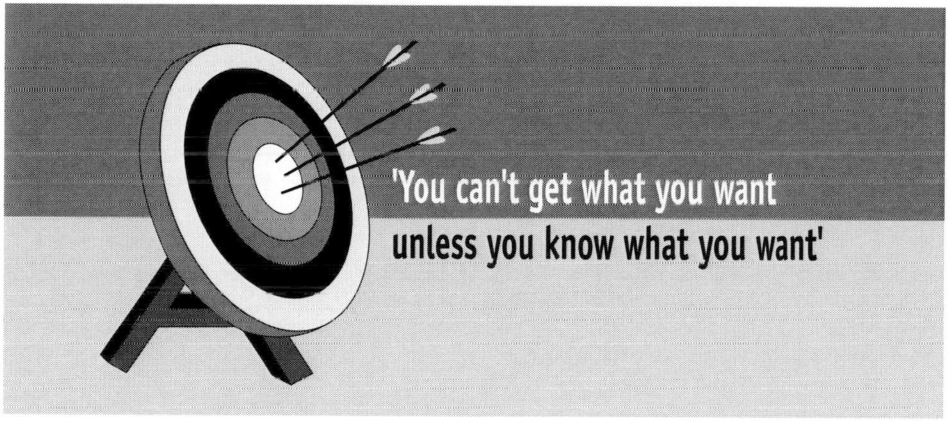

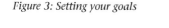

'You can't get what you want
unless you know what you want'

Figure 3: Setting your goals

Goals can take the form of lifetime objectives or daily targets. Each goal should be seen as a signpost on your journey of success and the effective setting of these goals is the single, most important activity that you will ever perform.

The effective setting of goals is the single, most important activity that you will ever perform

Key Learning Point

Goal setting procedure

The goal setting procedure is quite straight forward. You compile a list of wants, qualify them and convert them into goals. Seems simple enough, doesn't it? And it is. You start by making a dream list of all your wants or desires in the seven areas of your life without passing any judgement on your ability to achieve them. Psychologists will tell you that you use, at most, only 10 per cent of your true potential. In fact, the most recent brain research findings indicate that it is much lower-less than one per cent of your brain's capabilities! You are therefore in no position to accurately judge what you can or cannot accomplish. Include in your list both the personal qualities you wish to have as well as all the materialistic possessions you have ever dreamed of owning.

Rules for goal setting

There are five basic rules to be observed when embarking on an effective goal setting programme. Your goals should be:

a) Written

b) Challenging

c) Specific

d) Measurable

e) Prioritised

Written goals

Writing down your goals crystallises your thinking and creates personal commitment. Suppose, for example you wish to make extensions to your house or build a cottage in your ground. The likelihood of these plans materialising will be far greater if you were to sit down and produce a blueprint of the proposed design. Or, if you are responsible for doing the shopping on a monthly or weekly basis, you will know that your chances of returning home with everything you need, no more – no less, are much greater if you have a written list to follow. Some people will tell you they do not need to write down their goals. Why? It's in their heads – they know exactly what their goals are and by when they plan to achieve them. **NO** – they do not! They certainly think they do but they do not – and will not until they take the time and effort to put them down in writing. When they are written down they become much more clearly defined and the commitment to attain them is far greater than when they are merely vague ideas in the mind.

Lee Iacocca, in his autobiography, says: 'The discipline of writing something down is the first step toward making it happen. In conversations you can get away with all kinds of vagueness and nonsense, often without realising it. But there is something about putting your thoughts on paper that forces you to get down to specifics. That way, it's harder to deceive yourself – or anybody else.'

Yale University conducted an exercise, the results of which emphasise the power of written goals and plans. In a questionnaire handed to graduates of their 1953 class, the respondents were asked whether they had written goals and plans for their futures. Only 2.7 per cent (say three per cent) responded affirmatively. Twenty years later when a follow-up survey was carried out on the surviving graduates, it was found that the three per cent who had written goals and written plans to attain them had out-performed the other 97 per cent collectively in all areas of their lives! This is not to suggest that the three per cent had adhered rigidly to the written goals and plans that they had set originally. In fact, most of them had changed their goals, continuously resetting higher goals as existing ones were achieved. But they all attributed their successes to the process of habitually writing down their goals and plans of action to attain them.

Key Learning Point

Yale University findings: 'Twenty years later the three per cent who had written goals and plans had out-performed the other 97 per cent collectively in all areas of their lives'

Challenging goals

You are inherently a goal striving individual. Everybody is. That is apparent merely by studying history and observing the fact that every generation has progressed in goal achievement over the one before it. This is because challenges were met and the attainment of goals set newer and greater challenges. On an individual level, the very high goals that you should now have set for yourself need to be broken down into challenging sub-goals which have weekly targets and which you know, with a little effort on your part, you can obtain. This is a personal growth process. These challenges need to extend you just a little at first until you start developing the habit of accomplishing tasks, no matter how small. That starts building a success expectancy which will stimulate you to set yourself greater challenges. But it must start slowly – one step at a time.

Key Management Concept

Alfred P. Sloan, former president of General Motors, said that his guiding principle in establishing goals for his managers was: 'To make our standards difficult but possible to achieve as this is the most effective way of capitalising on the initiative, resourcefulness and capabilities of operating personnel.'

If you reflect on any significant achievement in your life, you will agree that the sense of satisfaction came from overcoming obstacles in the path to that goal. If the goals had been easily attainable, with relatively few obstacles to overcome your sense of satisfaction would have been considerably diminished. So the more challenging a goal can be to your initiative and resourcefulness, the greater the sense of satisfaction you will derive on its successful attainment.

The more challenging the goal – the greater the sense of satisfaction on its attainment

Incidentally, you will notice that none of the five rules for effective goal setting mentions that they should be 'realistic'. There is a very good reason for this. By asking yourself if your goals are realistic, you would need to become judgemental and would question, based on your past track record, whether or not you were capable of achieving the goals set. Remember that if you have only been using up to a maximum of 10 per cent of your potential you are in absolutely no position to judge what you can or cannot do. It is the strength of your desire and thus commitment that will determine your success – not your past performances.

Specific goals

You need to be as specific as possible in describing the goals you seek, for, as you repeat your goal statements at least three times a day, your subconscious mind needs clear, detailed pictures to work on. The more specific the goals, the more clarity these pictures will have and therefore the quicker they will be transformed into reality. Suppose you wanted a large family home with a lavish garden, expensive furniture, swimming pool, tennis court, double garage – all surrounded by a high wall. This description could fit any number of totally different homes. But, to define your goal, you must avoid generalities and be specific – in detail sufficient for you to picture it clearly in your mind's eye. Do that now. Assume that the home you had in mind was of Georgian style in a country setting. It has a large marble floor entrance hall leading to a magnificently appointed lounge with two crystal chandeliers overhanging Queen Anne style furniture, a mahogany half-moon bar in one corner with ten matching mahogany and leather upholstered bar stools. The long french windows, with sliding doors, open onto a wide patio with steps leading down to a sparkling, 50 ft long kidney shaped pool with change rooms and a sauna bath on the one side. On the other side of the pool is an all-weather floodlit tennis court with a spectators viewing pavilion. Do you get the picture? You must be able to accurately visualise exactly what you wish to have in the greatest possible detail.

Focused human potential is analogous to using a magnifying glass. We can take a box of sawdust or newspaper cuttings and leave them in the sun for days, weeks, months or even years without anything happening. However, the moment we take a magnifying glass and focus the rays of the sun, which were there all the time, we have a spark and then a fire. Taking it one step further, with modern technology we can concentrate the sun's diffused rays into a laser beam which can cut through steel or reinforced concrete. The same applies to human potential. When diffused or dissipated it accomplishes very little but when focused on a specific goal, it is tremendously effective. By directing the forces of your mind to a specific end, you will be harnessing the enormous power of focused attention which most people waste in spasmodic aimless thought.

Measurable goals

Your goals need to have some yardstick against which progress towards them can be measured. Wherever possible, therefore, quantify them and impose deadlines for their attainment. The sub-goals, which will form part of your plan of action should also be given target dates. Feedback is vital to developing self-confidence and fuelling the fire of desire which is so essential for success. Consequently, the more measurable the goals are, the more accurate the feedback and therefore the greater the prospects of the goals being attained by the set deadline. The establishment of measurable sub-goals creates a means of reinforcement. You are then constantly reminding yourself that you are indeed on track towards the attainment of your major goal. It's rather like travelling to a destination a long way away. The regular sign posts and distance markers provide the reinforcement feedback that you are on the right road.

Feedback is vital to developing self confidence and fuelling the fire of desire – so essential for success

Prioritised goals

The need to prioritise your goals is based on the fact that nobody can effectively accomplish more than one thing at a time. It is a basic time management principle to prioritise the tasks that you have to do and then concentrate your attention fully on the first one before moving onto the next. You will achieve far more this way than by trying to do a number of tasks at once.

You would think that airline pilots would not need to constantly refer to a prioritised checklist prior to landing or taking off as they must have done this on hundreds of occasions in the past. Yet the pilot and co-pilot methodically go through a series of checks in prioritised order to ensure that nothing is inadvertently overlooked which could have serious consequences. In the same way, by prioritising your goals in life you are able to focus on the important ones first and avoid dissipating your energy by attempting to tackle a number of goals simultaneously. There is an abundance of people who have the talent and ability to be successful but dissipate their energies by trying to do too many things at once. 'First Things First' is a useful motto to adopt when deciding on your action steps.

Cultivating belief

If you can clearly picture in your mind's eye your goal already attained and repeatedly recall that picture, then the working process of your subconscious mind begins to take over and find ways of directing you towards the satisfaction of that goal. Most books or tapes on goal setting will tell you that you need to believe that you have already achieved them. Quite so, but just telling you to believe that you have achieved them is one thing. Putting it into practice is another.

You cultivate the belief that you already have your goals fulfilled by utilisation of the affirmation technique coupled with regular visualisation and emotionalisation of these goals. Every day, at least three times a day, you should repeat the statements that you have written onto your goal cards. Additionally, twice a day, you engage in 20 minutes of autogenic conditioning, (see Chapter 1). This process starts to convince your subconscious mind that those goals have already been realised and, like any other habit, once it has sunk through into the subconscious mind, your goal directed actions become automatic.

Guide to Best Practice

The importance of repeating these affirmations to yourself and following up with visualisations and emotionalisations cannot be over stressed. This, in many cases is the difference between people succeeding and failing in life. They will embark on the procedure but only carry it out for a limited period of time because they do not see any immediate benefits. If you repeat the process continuously for 30 days, you will start to notice changes after just that one month – sometimes even sooner.

Rekindling desire

You must remember that if your desire for your goals is genuine, then the achievement of them is most definitely possible. If your desire starts to wane for any reason, you can resuscitate it by visualising the rewards and benefits that will accrue to you and your family once those goals have been fulfilled. The more often you carry out this visualisation exercise, the sooner will your desire be rekindled. The visualisation of your goals will be greatly facilitated by the construction of a goals poster. This would contain photographs, coloured pictures cut from magazines or brochures, or coloured drawings of the end results.

If your desire for your goals is genuine, then the achievement of them is most definitely possible

Power of choice

Og Mandino, undoubtedly one of the most widely read and respected Inspirational and self-help authors in the world, claims that the greatest power any individual has is the power of choice. You have that same power. You can choose the information to feed your subconscious mind which provides the motivation for the actions needed to satisfy your goals. Frederick Bailes in his book: *Your Mind Can Heal You* writes: 'Man's power of choice enables him to think like an angel or a devil, a king or a slave. Whatever the choices, mind will create and manifest.' Your life right now is the result of the past choices you have made. Similarly, your life in the future will be the result of the choices that you make from now onwards.

Changing goals

The world is constantly changing and you are along with it. Your values, perceptions and interests change and it follows that, in time, your goals may change too. That is not a reason to shirk goal setting. You have to be goal orientated if you are to realise your true potential. Never lower your goals. Where your desires and interests have altered and you wish to change your goals, always replace the original ones with higher goals. By all means change your plan, often if necessary, but never lower your goals. More about this in the next chapter.

Goal striving has to be enjoyable. Many believe that meaningful goal attainment only results from slavishly putting yourself through the mill day in and day out, sacrificing all the good things in life, so that one day in the far distant future, when the goal is reached, the rewards then will compensate for the sacrifices made now. That is absolute nonsense. Your success in life begins when you make the decision to become one of life's winners. This means living every day to its full – enjoying the journey – not just the destination. You need to regard goal setting as a progressively developmental process. To assist you, decide right now to be happy with what you have whilst pursuing what you want.

Key Learning Point

Your success in life begins when you make the decision to become one of life's winners

Pain and pleasure associations

Perhaps one of the reasons why you did not attain your goals in the past was because of the amount of pain you associated with them – probably subconsciously. You may have had a lot of conscious pleasure attached to the goal in the first place but could well have hindered your own progress by not being aware of, or not doing anything about, the (subconscious?) painful associations. You may have wanted to earn more money. If you are Mr/Mrs/Ms average then you certainly have the potential to do this. You undoubtedly reasoned that more money would give you greater freedom, enable you to do and buy all of the things you wanted and generally boost your level of happiness. However, if, simultaneously, you believed that having more money would alienate you from your friends or that family members would suddenly descend upon you for loans or that it might change you into an arrogant, manipulative type of person, then the chances are that you would find some way to frustrate your own attempts at acquiring more wealth.

To prevent possible sabotage of your steps towards your future goals, you need to identify any painful associations that might be lurking in your subconscious mind. The best way to do this is to write down whatever negative consequences you can consciously think of once the goal has been achieved. Then embark on 20 minutes of autogenic conditioning and both visualise and emotionalise the painful associations. You can now change the intensity by altering the picture you have conjured up. Change the colour of the picture to black and white; change the movie to a still frame; reduce the size to postage stamp dimensions; disassociate yourself from the picture – as though you were detached and seeing it on a separate screen. These alterations should certainly reduce the intensity of pain associated with the end result. You would then need to increase the intensity of the pleasurable emotions associated with the goal. A similar procedure is followed. Write down all the positive consequences you can consciously think of once the goal has been achieved. Then embark on another 20 minutes of autogenic conditioning, this time visualising and emotionalising the pleasurable associations. To increase the intensity of these emotions, make the picture bigger, more colourful, introduce more movement, become fully associated with the feelings by mentally transporting yourself into the picture and experiencing as vividly as possible, with as many senses as you can, the contentment, fulfilment and happiness that the achievement will bring.

Guide to Best Practice

Key Learning Point

Summary

1. You can't get what you want unless you know what you want – specifically.

2. Your subconscious mind is irrational, illogical and accepts as facts any suggestions continuously fed to it. It will not question whatever orders or instructions are given to it by the conscious mind but will carry them out slavishly whether they are positive or negative.

3. Programming yourself for success entails constantly projecting onto the screen of your subconscious mind pictures of the successful attainment of your goals, with everyone concerned enjoying the benefits and rewards of your achievements.

4. You cannot reap a harvest without first sowing the seeds. You can only realistically expect positive results to occur in your life when you consistently sow positive seeds which are the visualisations and emotionalisations of the end results that you desire.

5. Every habit you possess is a product of the conditioning of your subconscious mind.

6. The subconscious mind cannot differentiate between a real and a vividly imagined experience. This means that you can programme yourself with vividly imagined positive experiences which will have exactly the same effect, as far as the conditioning process is concerned, as actual experiences.

7. Regular use of autogenic conditioning (two sessions of 20 minutes each per day) will ensure that you remain passionate about your goals and retain a high level of motivation towards them.

8. The programming of your subconscious mind involves a regular schedule of affirmations, visualisations and emotionalisations of the goals you seek.

9. An essential prerequisite to effective goal setting is the establishment of a purpose in your life. Your purpose can be likened to a country's constitution or a company's mission statement, both of which portray values, standards or principles underneath which goals are set. Your most important values in life will determine your purpose.

10. Before commencing your journey of success, you need to know where you are. What resources do you possess? What strengths and weaknesses will help or hinder you?

11. To attain a balanced life, goals should be set in seven areas:

    a) Physical

    b) Mental

    c) Social

    d) Spiritual

    e) Personal

    g) Business

    f) Financial

12. The goal setting procedure involves compiling a list of wants, qualifying them and converting them into goals which are then transcribed onto 3"x 5" affirmation cards in the present tense as though they had already been achieved.

13. There are five basic rules to be observed when embarking on an effective goal setting programme.

    Your goals should be:

    a) Written

    b) Challenging

    c) Specific

    d) Measurable

    e) Prioritised

14. You cultivate the belief that you already have your goals fulfilled by utilisation of the affirmation technique coupled with regular visualisation and emotionalisation of the goals.

15. If your desire for your goals starts to wane for any reason, you can resuscitate it by visualising the rewards and benefits that will accrue to you and your family once those goals have been fulfilled.

16. The visualisation of your goals will be greatly facilitated by the construction of a goals poster displaying photographs, coloured pictures and drawings of the set goals.

17. Your life right now is the result of the past choices you have made. Similarly, your life in the future will be the result of the choices that you make from now onwards. Use the tremendous power of choice.

18. Change your goals (upwards) when your values, desires and interests change. Never change your goal because the plan did not work. Make a decision to be happy with what you have whilst pursuing what you want.

19. Remember that you may well have been sabotaging your own actions by virtue of the painful associations with the steps you have planned to take towards your goals. These can be overcome by autogenic conditioning.

If this is your first reading, please proceed to Chapter 3. If this is your second or subsequent reading, please carry out Activities 2, 3, 4, 5, 6, 7 and 8.

Activity No.2

Identifying your values

Values drive your life and you need to identify which ones are currently determining your behaviour. Listed on the following pages are 40 positive and 40 negative values. Go through each list ticking those values you believe are important (positive) and those you would most avoid (negative). Then go through the list again, this time giving a second tick to those values considered more important. Now repeat the exercise a third time allocating three ticks to your most important values. In the matrices provided, enter your ten most important positive values and ten most repelling negative values. Then, using the comparison table, compare your top five positive and negative values to determine any potential conflict which could be causing you to sabotage your own action steps towards your goals.

Positive values

Ask yourself: 'Which values are most important to me in my life?' Add your own if necessary.

Fairness	Support	Persistence	Freedom
Prosperity	Choice	Trustworthiness	Dedication
Honesty	Security	Loyalty	Attraction
Commitment	Competition	Success	Strength
Integrity	Adventure	Respect	Beauty
Friendship	Happiness	Compassion	Confidence
Determination	Enthusiasm	Challenge	Fun
Independence	Joy	Courage	Ecstasy
Love	Excitement	Growth	Creativity
Flexibility	Discipline	Spiritual Unity	Communication

Negative values

Ask yourself: 'Which of these values would I avoid the most?' Add your own if necessary.

Rejection	Anger	Humiliation	Worry
Depression	Regret	Misery	Sorrow
Frustration	Embarrassment	Despair	Poverty
Failure	Discouragement	Cynicism	Rigidity
Self-Doubt	Hostility	Pessimism	Sadness
Bitterness	Futility	Gloom	Resignation
Anxiety	Criticism	Despondency	Judgementation
Loneliness	Greed	Jealousy	Condemnation
Guilt	Lethargy	Suspicion	Fear of... (specify)
Disappointment	Ostracism	Withdrawal	Disinterest

Ranking your positive values

Positive values	A	B	C	D	E	F	G	H	I	J
1	▨									
2		▨								
3			▨							
4				▨						
5					▨					
6						▨				
7							▨			
8								▨		
9									▨	
10										▨

From the list of 40 positive values, choose 10 that you consider most important in your life. Enter these in the above matrix in alphabetical order both from 1 – 10 and from A – J. Now you can compare values with each other to establish your ranking order. You will be comparing your numbered values down the left hand side with the lettered values across the top. Start with the top row (No. 1) and move across the page from left to right, placing an X under each lettered column in which the value in the numbered row is currently more important to you than the one in the lettered column. For example, if the value in Row 1 is more important to you than the value in Column B place an X in the box where Row 1 and Column B intersect. If the value in Column B is more important then leave the box blank. Your most important positive values will then be those in the rows with the most Xs. Select your five top positive values and transfer them to the comparison table.

From the list of 40 negative values, choose 10 that you would do the most to avoid in your life. Enter these in the matrix opposite in alphabetical order both from 1-10 and from A-J. Now you can compare values with each other to establish your ranking order. You will be comparing your numbered values down the left hand side with the lettered values across the top. Start with the top row (No. 1) and move across the page from left to right, placing an X under each lettered column in which the value in the numbered row is currently more repelling (you would do more to avoid) than the one in the lettered column. For example, if the value in Row 1 is more repelling than the value in Column B, place an X in the box where Row 1 and Column B intersect. If the value in Column B is more repelling then leave the box blank. Your most important negative values will be those in the rows with the most Xs. Select your five top negative values, and transfer them to the comparison table on page 60.

Ranking your negative values

Negative values	A	B	C	D	E	F	G	H	I	J
1	▨									
2		▨								
3			▨							
4				▨						
5					▨					
6						▨				
7							▨			
8								▨		
9									▨	
10										▨

Comparing your positive and negative values

Rank	Positive	Negative
1		
2		
3		
4		
5		

1.   Enter your top five positive values established on the matrix.

2.   Do the same with your top five negative values.

3.   Now compare the lists to determine the degree of conflict (if any) that exists. For example, if your top positive value is 'Success' and your top negative value is 'Rejection' then you have a lot of potential conflict.

4.   Where there is conflict this must be resolved as, otherwise, you will sabotage your own action steps and your goals will elude you. The solution is to use your autogenic conditioning sessions and associate a lot of pain to the result of not taking the action steps you have decided upon and a lot of pleasure to the successful outcome once your action steps have been taken. You have to, initially, convince your brain to endure a certain amount of short-term pain (in the form of expenditure of time, effort or money) to ensure long-term pleasure.

Activity No. 3

Activity

Establishing your purpose in life

If you could write the inscription on your own tombstone, what would you like it to say?

_____

_____

For what would you best like to be remembered?

_____

_____

If you knew you could not fail, what would you do?

_____

_____

Statement of your main purpose in life:

_____

_____

Your reasons for having this as your main purpose in life are:

1. _____

_____

2. _____

_____

3. _____

_____

Activity

Activity No. 4

Where am I now?

Answer the following questions as honestly as you can. The answers will give you a clear picture of where you are right now – the starting point on your journey of success. You must know exactly where you are before you set off for where you want to be.

1. Did you set goals for yourself five years ago depicting where you wanted to be today? If YES, have you achieved them all? If not, do you know why not?

2. In the past have you used any of the following EXCUSES as 'reasons' for not achieving your goals?

    – lacked ability (or intelligence, education, experience)

    – lacked opportunity

    – lacked money

    – lacked time

    – lacked desire (or drive)

    – lacked support of family or friends

    If you used one or more of the above excuses for not taking action, don't feel bad. You're in good company. In fact, you are part of the majority but it need not remain that way if you (and you alone) are prepared to assume responsibility for your future and commit yourself to becoming an achiever. You must start by eradicating all these excuses from your thinking/belief system. Replace them with empowering beliefs. (See Activity No. 23 page 168).

3. What have you accomplished over the last year that you are really proud of? Think of the things you wanted to do a year ago and on a scale of 0-10 give yourself

an overall accomplishment rating. A score of five or more indicates you achieved at least half of the goals set a year ago, which is way above average. A score of four or less requires an explanation, which may be found in the second question!

4.   What are the most important roles that you play in your life (e.g. wife, mother, husband, father, gardener, gymnast, sportsman/woman, businessman/woman, friend etc)? Have you in the past set yourself goals for each of the roles you play? If YES, are you satisfied with your progress towards them? If not, what do you intend to do about it?

My most important roles and goals are:

Role   **Goals**

_____

_____

_____

_____

5.   What lessons have you learned from your past successes and 'failures' that will help you achieve your future goals?

_____

_____

_____

_____

You are now ready to take stock of the resources you possess which will help you achieve your goals. See Activity No. 5.

Activity No. 5

Your personal resources

Are you fully aware of the resources you possess? Go through the list below and tick all of the resources that apply to you. Add any of your own which do not appear on the list. Then go through the list a second time ticking twice those more important. Repeat a third time giving three ticks to those considered most important.

Skills:

Literacy

Numeracy

Typing

Filing

Shorthand

Report and letter writing

Office administration

Leading groups

Counselling others

Selling ability

Negotiating ability

Public speaking

Decision making

Manual dexterity

Playing musical instruments

Analytical

Foreign languages

Artistic ability

Innovative/creative

Knitting/sewing

Design sense

Flying

Carpentry

Academic qualifications

Hairdressing

Diving

Sporting ability (sport: _____)

Objectivity

Entertaining

Cooking

Other (specify)

Personal qualities:

Determination	Good health
Sense of responsibility	Kindness
Self-confidence	Self-motivated
Reliability	Gregariousness
Conscientiousness	Sound judgement
Persuasiveness	Persistence
Honesty	Tact
Courage	Charm
Enthusiasm	Concentration
People orientated	Articulation
Patience	Perception
Resourcefulness	Intelligence
Cheerfulness	Self-management ability
Ambition	Positive attitude
Instinctiveness	Willpower
Sympathy	Passion
Tenacity	Others (specify)
Energy	

Rank your top five skills and qualities in order of importance.

Skills

1. _____

2. _____

3. _____

4. _____

5. _____

Qualities

1. _____

2. _____

3. _____

4. _____

5. _____

Money

Calculate the amount of money you are prepared to invest in yourself and your plan to attain your goals. Include your initial capital outlay (set-up costs) and then your regular monthly amounts.

1. Initial capital outlay:

2. Monthly investment:

Time

How much time are you committed to making available per day/week/month to follow your goal plans?

Supportive environment

List the relatives, friends, business colleagues or associates who could be supportive in helping you to achieve your goals. Do you admire and respect someone who could become your mentor?

Relatives:

_____

_____

Friends:

_____

_____

Business colleagues:

_____

_____

Mentor:

_____

_____

When do you plan to contact them to discuss your goals?

Diarise this now!

Activity

Current balance status in the seven areas of your life

Is your life well balanced? Here is a simple exercise to answer that question. The diagram below represents your wheel of life with each of the seven spokes depicting an area of your life. On a scale of 0-10, rate your degree of satisfaction in each area, 0 being completely dissatisfied and 10 being completely satisfied with the degree of goal attainment in that area. Then join the seven points. This will highlight any areas of imbalance which you may then choose to rectify.

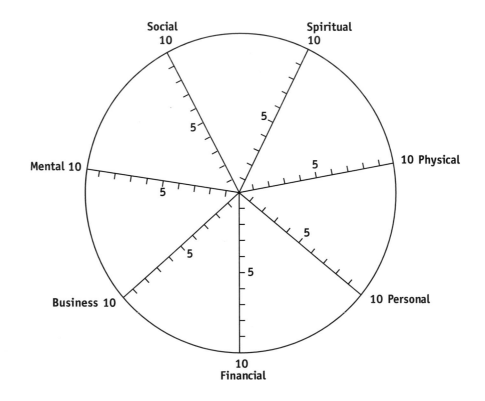

Activity No. 7

Establishing your desires

The objective of this activity is to assist you in determining what you will be, do or have in the future.

Go through the list of suggested desires and tick each one with an 'A', 'B' or 'C' depending upon whether you have a burning desire for it ('A'), it is important to you ('B') or is of little or no interest to you ('C').

On a separate sheet of paper write down, in full, every one of the desires which you have ticked as 'A'. (The act of writing them down in longhand clarifies your thinking and re-inforces your desire for them.) Now do the same for those you have ticked as 'B'. Use a separate sheet of paper.

Ignore those you have ticked as 'C'. They play no further part in this exercise.

Now go through your list of 'B's and ask yourself whether any of them could become 'A's. In other words, whilst they may be important to you, you do not currently have a burning desire for them but believe that you could develop this in the future. Add any 'B's which could become 'A's to your 'A' list.

Take your consolidated 'A' list and against each one of your desires place a 1, 3, 5, 10 or 10+ representing the time in years by when this desire will be fulfilled.

Now, irrespective of the time factor, choose your four most important goals and rank them in order of importance:

My four most important goals are:

1. _____

2. _____

3. _____

4. _____

If any of the four goals have a deadline for achievement in excess of one year, determine the sub-goals that need to be attained within the next year:

The sub-goals that I am going to attain by _____ are :

1. _____

2. _____

3. _____

4. _____

5. _____

6. _____

7. _____

8. _____

9. _____

10. _____

11. _____

12. _____

Suggested desires	A	B	C
Have a secure job			
Earn all the money I can			
Save more money			
Win recognition for myself			
Have a new car			
Make a new friend			
Attend a seminar			
Listen to an educational tape			
Enhance my marriage			
Become closer to my children			
Quit smoking			
Learn another language			
Lose weight			
Gain weight			
Earn a college degree			
Have more money for investment			
Work with my hands			
Work with my head			
Serve others			
Learn to ski, scuba-dive, sky-dive or other activity			
Lead others			
Help a favourite charity			
Feel 'down' less often			
Be a good team member			

A = This is a **burning desire** – vital to my personal success.

B = This is **important** – it is something I would 'like to' rather than 'must' be, do or have.

C = This is of little or no interest at all to me.

Suggested desires	A	B	C
Participate in sports			
Cold canvass			
Close a sale			
Make appointments			
Give an excellent presentation			
Keep business records			
Start a conversation with people I don't know			
Perform a personal service			
Work for the community			
Help the handicapped			
Buy a franchise			
Own a boat or yacht			
Sell intangibles			
Sell tangibles			
Complete whatever I start			
Have more time for hobbies/interests			
Learn to apologise sincerely when I'm at fault			
Take three holidays a year			
Flirt more effectively			
Buy expensive clothes			
Play a musical instrument			
Conduct an interesting dinner party conversation			
Go on a 'round the world' tour			
Not feel under pressure at work			
Pass an examination – specify			
Get a job I enjoy more			

A = This is a **burning desire** – vital to my personal success.

B = This is **important** – it is something I would 'like to' rather than 'must' be, do or have.

C = This is of little or no interest at all to me.

Suggested desires	A	B	C
Deal better with boring people			
Go on a safari			
Stand up for myself more often			
Feel in less of a rut			
Acquire a pet			
Get on better with my brothers/sisters			
Be a better host/hostess			
Live in the country			
Enjoy a better sex life			
Get promoted at work			
Be fitter			
Learn to say 'no' when appropriate			
Get on better with my parents			
Come across better in meetings			
Not feel bored			
Use my travelling/commuting time better			
Ask for what I want			
Learn to dance			
Have a holiday home			
Handle criticism better			
Feel more confident			
Have more shared interests with my partner			
See more films/plays			
Be appreciated more at work			
Earn money in my spare time			
Learn to fly			

A = This is a **burning desire** – vital to my personal success.

B = This is **important** – it is something I would 'like to' rather than 'must' be, do or have.

C = This is of little or no interest at all to me.

Suggested desires	A	B	C
Educate my children			
Buy a better home			
Retire with a guaranteed income			
Travel			
Be on a TV show			
Create a business from scratch			
Buy a going business			
Develop my own ideas			
Write a book			
Read a book			
See a movie			
Be director of a company			
Be president of a civic club			
Be free of debts			
Have good health and more energy			
Be a film star			
Cut a hit record			
Win an award – specify:			
Obtain security for family			
Acquire personal security			
Work regular hours			
Work my own hours			
Own a second home			

A = This is a **burning desire** – vital to my personal success.

B = This is **important** – it is something I would 'like to' rather than 'must' be, do or have.

C = This is of little or no interest at all to me

Activity No. 8

Compiling your own 'dream' list

Using the spaces provided compile a 'dream' list in each one of the seven goal setting areas (physical, mental, social, spiritual, personal, business, financial). Assume that you had unlimited financial resources, abilities, and time. Allow your brain to free-wheel. Write down everything you have ever wanted from life.

Having listed your wants in all seven areas, pose two questions to each want:

1. Will it contribute to the fulfillment of my main purpose in life?

2. Do I have, or can I arouse a burning desire to achieve this?

The second question is most important as the achievement of any one of your goals will be directly related to the amount of desire that you can arouse for it.

Once those two questions have been answered honestly and you have disqualified a number of your wants, you are now ready to convert the qualified ones into goals. You do this by writing your qualified wants, onto 3" x 5" cards, in the present tense as though they had already been achieved. The reason for this is because you are going to repeat these goal statements, or affirmations, to your subconscious mind regularly, (three times a day, initially) which will, in time, create a positive expectancy of and confident belief in your personal success.

Now that you have your goals written onto the cards, you should go through them and prioritise them according to your own values of importance. Ask yourself the question: 'What is most important to me in this particular area of my life?' Once you have established the top priority goal then move on to the next and so on until you have prioritised all the goals in that particular area. Carry out this exercise in all of your goal areas. It will pay you to regularly review this priority list as some goals could well gain in importance and leapfrog over others on your list. Initially, revise the list once a week. After a few weeks this can be converted into a monthly review.

Next, you should select the top priority goals in each area and carry these cards with you everyday. You should read these over to yourself (aloud, if possible) at least three times a day in order to imprint them on your subconscious mind.

There is no hard and fast rule for the number of goals which you should be pursuing at any one time. This will very much depend on the degree of difficulty of the individual goals. However, remember the benefits of focus. You will always achieve more by focusing your attention on one goal to start with and only on completion of that goal moving on to the next one. Nevertheless, it is possible during the course of a day to spend time on several goals in different areas and you will soon develop a feel for the number of goals that you can comfortably pursue at any one time. (On the Personal Success Coaching Programmes that I conduct, we work on four goals every 90 day period.)

'Dream' list of physical wants

'Dream' list of mental wants

'Dream' list of social wants

'Dream' list of spiritual wants

'Dream' list of personal wants

'Dream' list of business wants

'Dream' list of financial wants

How to plan to attain your goals

Chapter 3

One of the traps people fall into is having their goals and subsequent plans of action outside their control or area of responsibility. The success of their plans depends upon the decisions of others. Consequently, when things do not quite go according to plan they have a ready made 'cop-out'. We must take responsibility for our own lives and, as part of this responsibility, ensure that the action steps we have outlined in order to achieve our goals are within our control.

Key Learning Point

We must ensure that the action steps to achieve our goals are within our control

A goal can be likened to a destination. Once you have decided on your destination, you need to determine how you are going to get there. This is where planning enters the picture. A goal without planning is just a dream which often becomes a nightmare when progress towards it is frustrated. Planning does not guarantee the successful attainment of the goal but certainly increases your chances immensely of getting there.

Key Question

How do I get there?

Planning has been described as 'thinking before doing'. It means working out in advance the activities that have to be performed to obtain your goals. Most people's personal goals are achieved either haphazardly or systematically. You may get results if you are very lucky or extremely capable by plunging blindly ahead trying to solve problems as they arise and taking advantage of opportunities along the way. But the average man or woman is neither lucky enough nor capable enough to achieve the desired results by adopting this hit-or-miss approach. So some form of planning becomes necessary – the thinking through of what you want to accomplish and how best you are going to do it.

Written plans form the basis of successful action. You have the ability to master your own future and you can make happen what you want to happen provided you decide in advance what you are going to do, how you are going to do it and what you will need to do it.

Flexibility

Guide to Best Practice

The key word in any planning process is 'flexibility'. Many people become so anxious over how they are going to reach their goals that they never take the first step. Simply because a clear-cut path does not magically appear before them, they avoid spending time on creative thinking to determine what action steps are necessary. Whilst planning is very important, keeping in mind clearly defined pictures of your final goal is absolutely vital to your eventual success. Plans can and should change as circumstances change. However, all too often in life, people tend to change their goal (usually lowering it) rather than changing their plan to attain it. 'Many roads lead to Rome', is an oft-quoted saying. The mere fact that you may have gone down a cul-de-sac is no reason for you to accept that as the end of your progress towards your original destination. You merely need to turn around, retrace your steps and try another road. That is what is meant by flexibility. If one plan fails, it does not mean that the goals are unattainable. It simply means that the plan, for those particular circumstances, is not completely satisfactory and needs changing.

Never change the goal because the plan did not work – change the plan!

Key Learning Point

Interested or committed?

If you have ever taken your family or relatives away on holiday, then you will have been involved in the planning process. It would, no doubt, have been most enjoyable as you probably involved other members of your family and you would all have become enthusiastic because you could visualise yourselves enjoying that holiday. Unfortunately, it is a sad fact that most people spend more time planning their annual holiday than they ever do planning for the most important trip of their lives – their journey of success through the realisation of their true potential. Planning is regarded as essential when embarking on any long journey and you should regard success as a journey rather than a destination. In your planned journey to your holiday destination you would pass towns, villages and landmarks which would act, as do the national road signs as indicators of your progress. It is the same with self-development. Whilst your goal is your destination, you need signposts along the way to show how you are progressing. You must establish these signposts, or stepping stones towards your goals as part of your plan and then commit yourself to achieving them.

Key Learning Point

You should regard success as a journey rather than a destination

At this point let me stress that there is a big difference between interest in a goal and commitment to it. Take financial independence as an example. Most people would agree that they are interested in becoming financially independent. But how many are committed to achieving it? Only between three and eight per cent. How about that for a sobering statistic? Less than eight per cent of those wishing to become financially independent actually make it. The ones who make it do so because they have commitment rather than just interest. They are able to spontaneously answer you with clear, specific, detailed reasons when you ask 'Why?' That is the difference. A committed person knows why he is doing what he is doing. Someone who is merely interested would have difficulty answering your question because he has not delved deeply enough into his reasons for wanting the goal – he has not internalised the goal sufficiently to be emotionally fired up about it. Commitment to your goal therefore, is absolutely essential. It means that your goal must be so clearly

Guide to Best Practice

imprinted on your mind and your desire to achieve it so intense, that all your efforts are directed towards its attainment. Half measures are no good. Your commitment must be total and if your goal is one that you genuinely desire, it will be. Nobody ever reached second base by keeping one foot in first. Commitment means going for your goal with everything you have. You must be prepared to leave your existing comfort zone to pursue new levels of achievement. You may well make mistakes along the way – after all, you are human. The only people who do not make mistakes are those who refuse to attempt anything but then, of course, they are making the biggest mistake of all – failure to use their abilities. You should not be scared of making mistakes – when they occur see them as learning experiences so essential to your personal growth and goal attainment.

Annual goals

Most successful businesses will have five year plans which are reviewed and changed when necessary every year. This enables them to look to the future, to visualise the position their company will be in after so many years. But the five year plan is not enough. It is far too long-term to be an effective motivational tool for the day to day running of the business. This is achieved by annual planning where all departments are involved in the setting of budgets, which will reflect the anticipated sales, cost of sales, expenses and profit for the forthcoming year. The budget is broken down into monthly figures showing how much is intended to be spent on what and when and how much is expected to be received over the same period. The budget acts not only as the business forecast for the year but also the means of control, of seeing just where actual results differ from those expected. Wherever negative discrepancies arise, management can investigate the causes and take action to prevent recurrences. Similarly, where actual results are better than predicted, management

Key Management Concept

is in a position to take full advantage of the situation. A budget forms the basis for the development of programmes which describe the action steps to be taken by each department to accomplish their objectives. These programmes, or schedules, are the result of thinking through the best ways to reach the goals set and establishing both the time sequence and the priority for each activity. The budget also allocates company resources to the different departments, to enable them to play their part in carrying out the annual plan.

Your individual plan needs to follow a similar process – use the same principles as do the successful businesses. Work out where you want to be in five years time. Then break that down into annual goals and quarterly sub-goals. You are then in a position to develop your action plan

Activity

Work out where you want to be five years from now. Divide that goal into five annual goals and the first annual goal into quarterly sub-goals. You are then in a position to develop your action plan

Guide to Best Practice

Planning process

The first step in the planning process is to take a clean sheet of paper and at the top write in your number one prioritised goal statement. Next you need to decide what you are going to give in return for this goal. You must realise that you will get nothing for nothing in life and any achievement is a direct reflection of what you have put in. You must, therefore, determine what sacrifices in terms of time, effort and money you are prepared to make in order to achieve that goal. Of course if it is, as it should be, a goal which you genuinely desire, then the amount of time, effort and money which you are prepared to sacrifice will be considerable, because this will indicate your degree of commitment and, as already mentioned, without commitment the chances of obtaining your goal are fairly remote.

Sub-goals and deadlines

Once you have set aside a specific amount of time each day, particularly at weekends and if need be a certain amount of money that you are prepared to invest in the attainment of this goal, you can now divide your main goal into sub-goals. You want to know how you are progressing at any time and setting sub-goals with deadlines for each one creates check points along the way. Norman Vincent Peale, in his classic book: *The Power of Positive Thinking*, exhorts the reader to: 'Plan your work – work your plan'. This is excellent advice if only it were heeded.

Plan your work – work your plan

Setting deadlines to your plan evokes commitment to following it. Having deadlines shows how you are progressing and meeting them reinforces your motivation. Additionally, they force you to concentrate your attention on the subject concerned whether you feel like it or not. We human beings are great procrastinators and will find numerous excuses not to do something when we do not quite feel in the mood. But, when deadlines have been set and we have to get down to it, our mood, more often than not, soon changes and both our interest in the subject being studied and our motivational drive will be rekindled. It would be ludicrous for any business to develop a plan, a budget or set objectives without deadlines for their attainment. It is even more important for you to place deadlines on your personal objectives in life. Deadlines will help you to 'work your plan'.

Key Learning Point

Creative thinking

Having established your sub-goals ask yourself: 'What is preventing me from achieving them?' List the obstacles you can foresee in your path and the possible solutions to overcome them. You may find that you cannot immediately come up with alternative solutions to the obstacles. Don't worry. Do some creative thinking – engage in a personal brain-storming session where you allow your mind to freewheel without any preconceived constraints. Write down all of the ideas that spring to mind. One or more of them could prove to be the practical solution you are seeking. If you do not have success after the first couple of sessions, keep trying. The more creative thinking (autogenic conditioning) you carry out, the more ideas will be generated. You can also ask others for their advice on the subject but be sure to ask only those who are likely to have the answers by virtue of their professional past experience and who are willing to help you. Do not, for instance, ask financial investment advice from your plumber or butcher. (That is not to suggest that you would not get advice – you probably would, but you want to be certain of the value of that advice!)

Obstacles

In preparing your plan of action, you need to identify the obstacles which could hinder your progress and then to determine ways of overcoming them. It is useful at this stage to mentally convert the word 'obstacle' into 'challenge'. Once you can see your challenges as opportunities to grow and realise that the more challenges you have in life the stronger you become and the better equipped you are to handle greater challenges, your attitude will change and you will actually welcome the challenges when they arise.

Key Learning Point

'Obstacles' in the path to your goals provide the opportunities for personal growth

Written goals and plans

Once you have alternative solutions to overcoming the obstacles listed, decide upon the one which you feel has the best chance of success. This will form the basis of your action steps. Write them down as part of your plan. Notice the emphasis on having your plan as well as your goal in writing. By writing out your goal statements and the plan of action, you will be developing the habit of crystallising your thinking and refining your desires. This process focuses your attention fully on where you want to go and prevents the vagueness of goals which many people have. Committing your goals and plans to paper is essential – it may seem burdensome to start with, but after a while when you notice the tremendous benefits which ensue, you will appreciate the reasons for it.

The establishing of intermediate or sub-goals and deadlines for their attainment should be carried out right down to weekly and even daily goals. You need to live in day tight compartments because, if you focus on the present and concentrate on being successful in whatever actions you are performing right at this very moment, then you will make rapid progress towards your goals. On the other hand, working for a long-term objective, without having broken that down into the sub-goals can often be very frustrating. When obstacles are encountered to which solutions can't readily be found, the tendency is to lose interest in that goal and start rationalising that you did not really desire it anyway. Remember, *never change the goal because the plan did not work*. Rather, treat the 'failure' as the negative feedback that it is and learn from it with a view to revising your plan of action.

You will also encounter obstacles which you had not predicted. The most important consideration here is your attitude towards them. Successful people accept obstacles as being inevitable but regard them as challenges which must be faced – as opportunities to grow. They know that the best way to overcome them is to confront them, look at them objectively and search for ways around them because, in the words of W. Clement Stone: *'Any adversity carries within it the seed of an even greater benefit.'* Welcome the resistance that these obstacles offer you.

The situation is analogous to a man wishing to develop his body. He can spend hours, days, even weeks reading manuals, looking at pictures in magazines and books, watching films and videos, listening to tapes and discussing the subject with bodybuilding instructors. Until he actually goes into action and starts lifting weights or using the resistance of the machines to act against his muscles, he will not start to develop his body.

In exactly the same way the successful person needs obstacles and actually welcomes them because they give him opportunities to grow, to use the talents and abilities he possesses and discover his creativity in overcoming them. So be grateful for whatever problems arise and then tackle them in the firm belief that you are going to overcome them and as a result, grow from them. Remember you don't drown by falling into water. You only drown if you stay there! When obstacles arise, confront them, break them down into smaller pieces and then tackle each piece one at a time and you will soon see that the apprehension that you had at the outset turns into satisfaction from achievement and you are now in a better position to welcome the next one. As each little piece of the problem is overcome, you are reinforcing the picture of yourself as a winner. Every success, no matter how small plays a part in influencing your subconscious mind, enhancing your self-confidence and creating a success expectancy.

A major characteristic of successful achievers is persistence. Any plan can have it's shortcomings – you may find that you come up against obstacles which you cannot readily resolve. That does not mean that you cannot get around them. You must not see your plans as being etched in stone and unchangeable. Your goals should remain constant and single minded but your plan can change, even daily if necessary. The person who persists, who keeps his goal in mind and constantly searches for ways of overcoming the obstacles in his path will surely find the way. Napoleon Hill puts it so well in his quotation: 'Quitters never win – winners never quit.' With persistence you can overcome all obstacles providing your desire is genuine and you have the necessary commitment to go after your goal.

Rewards and benefits

You are now ready for the final phase of your plan of action – to write out in full the benefits and rewards on successful attainment of your goals. The reason for this is fairly straight forward. The achievement of any goal is directly related to the amount of desire that can be aroused for it. Any worthwhile goal will have numerous obstacles in its path. This is understandable as it would neither provide any satisfaction nor be regarded as a noteworthy success if the goal were easily attainable. It is like a high jumper going out for the first time and putting the bar a couple of centimetres from the ground and jumping over it. There would be no sense of achievement in that. However, when the bar is at a height which provides a challenge and when that is overcome, the satisfaction derived from that achievement provides positive reinforcement and the motivation to overcome even greater challenges. However, often these obstacles are not overcome as quickly or as easily as you would like them to be. The danger then exists that your desire, your intense interest in obtaining the goal, may start to wane. This is the time when you would consult your rewards and benefits column in your plan of action and rekindle that desire. It also assists in the autogenic conditioning that you will be doing twice a day. It forms a vital part of your plan of action.

Perhaps you feel that you do not have the determination to stick to your plan. Maybe you do not right now, but you will. That is what this book is all about – *changing your life for the better* – developing and improving those qualities necessary for the attainment of your goals. Go ahead and make out your plans to attain your goals without any inhibiting thoughts. Correct planning will retain your interest and enthusiasm at a high level. Everyone knows that the future is uncertain but you must not allow that uncertainty to control your present actions. Instead, you stand the best chance of controlling your own future by the deliberate setting of goals and development of plans to achieve them. If you want to create the sort of future that, up till now, you have merely dreamt about, then planning must become an integral part of your changing process.

Key Learning Point

You stand the best chance of controlling your own future by the deliberate setting of goals and development of plans to achieve them

Key Learning Points

Summary

1. Your plans must be within your area of control and not depend on the decisions of others.

2. The key word in any planning process is flexibility.

3. Never change the goal because the plan did not work – change the plan!

4. Only between three and at most eight per cent of people achieve financial independence – a goal desired by virtually everyone. The ones who have achieved it have realised that interest is never enough. It has to be transformed into commitment. Without commitment to the goals and plans, success will remain out of reach.

5. A committed person has sufficiently compelling reasons for doing what he is doing. Commitment means sustaining a strong enough desire through regular autogenic conditioning to risk leaving your comfort zone in order to scale new heights.

6. Effective planning involves the breaking down of long-term goals into short-term sub-goals with deadlines for their attainment. The action steps required to reach each sub-goal are then determined.

7. 'Plan your work – work your plan'. Setting deadlines to your sub-goals enhances your commitment to following your plan.

8. Part of the planning process involves listing all the obstacles that you can see in your path. The solutions to these obstacles form the action steps of your plan and where the solutions are not readily apparent, you need to engage in regular creative thinking (autogenic conditioning) to generate ideas towards overcoming these obstacles.

9. The process of regularly writing out your goal statements and the plans of action to attain them is essential if you are to attain meaningful success.

10. Where obstacles are encountered to which solutions do not quickly come to mind, despite your creative thinking, your attitude towards your situation is all important. You must cultivate the attitude of seeing every obstacle as a learning experience – as an opportunity to grow. Break the obstacles down into smaller pieces and then tackle each piece one at a time.

11. The achievement of any goal is directly related to the amount of desire that can be aroused for it. As part of your plan of action you need to write out in full the benefits and rewards that will accrue to you and your loved ones on successful attainment of your goals. To sustain your desire at a high level, you would refer to these rewards and benefits on a daily basis (i.e. twice a day when carrying out your autogenic conditioning sessions).

If this is your first reading, please proceed to Chapter 4. If this is your second or subsequent reading, please carry out Activities 9, 10, 11 and 12.

Activity No. 9

Plan of action: Major goals and sub-goals

For each of your four major goals, you now need to compile a Plan of Action. On the page opposite, enter in your major goal statements and the deadlines for their accomplishment. Then divide each major goal into sub-goals which should be listed with their respective deadlines. You can now devise a plan to attain each sub-goal remembering to prioritise them correctly so that the attainment of one becomes the springboard to the next.

List all the obstacles that are hindering or preventing you from attaining the sub-goal. (There will obviously be certain obstacles that do not spring to mind immediately. Enter these onto your plan as and when they arise.) Now, for every obstacle listed, decide on a solution (activity) that will overcome the obstacle and alongside put in the time by when you intend completing that action step.

Finally, write down the rewards and benefits of successful attainment of the major goal – how you will feel, how your loved ones will feel and how your life will change once it has been achieved.

Plan of action: Major goals

Major goal No.	Description of major goal to be achieved	Completion date

Plan of action: Sub-goals

Major goal ref.	Sub-goal No.	Description of sub-goal to be achieved	Completion date

Produce your own sheets in the above format where required.

Plan of action

Major goal No. _____ with completion deadline:			
Sub-goal No:			
Deadline:			
List of obstacles:			
No.	Obstacle	No.	Obstacle

Solutions to obstacles (action steps)

Obstacle No.	Solution (action steps)	Deadline

Produce your own sheets in the above format for additional sub-goals.

Rewards and benefits on successful attainment

1. How will you feel once this goal has been attained?

2. How will your loved ones feel once you have achieved this goal?

3. How will your life change once you have achieved this goal?

Produce your own sheets in the above format for additional major goals.

Activity No. 10

Rewriting goals and plans
(Establishing and maintaining focus)

This activity requires you to write out in long hand every day for the next 30 days your four major goal statements and the plans of action which you have formulated to attain them. Ideally, every day you should write your major goal statements and plans without referring to the previous day's refined version. If you are carrying out autogenic conditioning sessions twice a day for 20 minutes a time, the ideas on how to attain your goals should be coming thick and fast. Consequently, every time that you write down your goals and plans there may well be some changes. At the end of the 30 day period there should be absolutely no doubt in your mind as to what you want to be, do or have regarding the four major goals you have set, your reasons for wanting them and exactly how you plan to go about attaining them. This activity will ensure you are constantly focused on what it is you want and are not easily distracted into thinking about what you do not want.

Activity No. 11

Construction of your goals poster

A practical aid to both visualising your goals and keeping them constantly in mind is a goals poster.

Construct your own goals poster by taking a large piece of cardboard or thick paper, drawing or cutting out coloured pictures from magazines or brochures of the goals you seek and glueing them onto your poster. Do this for your four major goals to start with and, as a goal is attained, replace it on your poster with another.

Next to the picture of your goal insert brief information or statistics from your plan of action. For example, if your goal was to lose weight, your goal picture would represent how you will look at your ideal weight which would be written next to the picture together with the deadline date and how you plan to achieve it (e.g. exercise – 40 minutes aerobics, five times a week. Diet – high water content – fruits, salads and fresh vegetables).

Your completed goals poster should then be hung in a prominent position where it will provide a constant reminder of what you are going to be, do or have. It assists in obtaining right and left brain congruency. The pictures, patterns, colours, layout (spatial representation), all activate the right brain whilst the words, numbers, symbols and time provide left brain stimulation.

Activity No. 12

Monthly and weekly plans

Refer to your plans of action for your four major goals (Activity No. 9). For each one of your four major goals, choose a sub-goal you plan to have attained one month from now.

For each sub-goal list the activities that need to be performed and the approximate time you plan to spend on each activity, then prioritise these activities. Now decide what objectives you plan to have accomplished in one week's time and transfer the relevant activities from your weekly plan onto your monthly plan.

Once you have transferred all the activities relating to all four sub-goals then re-prioritise and allocate certain activities to particular days.

Monthly plan

Major goal No. ___ : _____

Sub-goal to be attained one month from today: _____

Activities to be performed to reach sub-goal	Approx time reqd	Priority

Use this format for each of your four major goals.

Weekly plan

Objectives (What I plan to have accomplished by the end of the week)

_____

_____

_____

_____

_____

_____

_____

_____

_____

_____

Activities (Required to accomplish the above objectives)	Priority	Time needed	Day

How to manage your time

Chapter 4

Now that you have set your goals and started to establish a plan of action for achieving them, you will need to know how to manage your time more effectively, as this forms the basis of meaningful planning.

Time is a resource. But, unlike other resources, it cannot be saved, borrowed or exchanged. It can only be spent. And yet, surprisingly, most of us tend to look for ways of saving it rather than spending it more productively.

Key Question

Are you activity or accomplishment orientated?

Key Learning Point

Suppose I were to make you an offer of giving you £86,400 every day. The only stipulation was that you would have to spend it, because whatever you did not spend, you lost. I am sure you would find numerous ways of spending it all, wouldn't you? It is exactly the same with time. We have 86,400 seconds to spend everyday of our life. Consider, for a moment, what you are doing with that time. Are you spending it correctly? An excellent book by Alan Lakein entitled, *How to Get Control of Your Time and Your Life* contains a statement that sets the tone for positive time management. He says that: 'Making the right choices about how you use your time, is more important than doing efficiently whatever job happens to be around.' So many people go through the motions of being very efficient. They usually are – at shuffling papers. They are not really achieving objectives. In short, they are not effective. They are confusing activity with accomplishment.

Key Management Concept

Time management – a skill

You will often hear people claim that there are not enough hours in a day to do the things that they would like to do. This is very rarely the case. More often than not it is a question of the time available not being used to proper effect.

Using time to your best advantage is a skill that can be developed, much the same as any other skill, such as typing or driving your motor car. Effective time management will not give you any more time in your life, but will certainly help you to spend the time available to you much more productively.

'To Do' list

Guide to Best Practice

One of the secrets of getting things done is to compile a daily 'To Do' list. Og Mandino, who was the editor of the magazine *Success Unlimited* for 15 years and had opportunities to interview numerous successful top entrepreneurs, found a common trait amongst most of them. This was that they regularly used a 'To Do' list. There is nothing revelationary about this and, in present times, this is certainly not a new innovation. In fact, most people have heard of and know how to compile such a list. However, knowing something and putting it into practice are two different things entirely and, as we are natural procrastinators, we often never get around to effectively introducing it into our lives. All that is needed, is to take a few minutes, preferably at the end of each day, writing down the *six*, (and try to make it no more than six) of the most important activities that need to be performed the next day, then prioritise them A, B or C, A being vital – it must be done today, B being important – it should be done today and C being unimportant – it could be done once all the A's and B's have been completed. Then prioritise the As, Bs and Cs numerically on their relative degrees of importance. Now allocate to each task a time which you feel will be sufficient for its completion. Then, the next morning, clear your desk or work area of everything except the information and materials relating to the number one prioritised item and work on this until it is completed. Do not start on any of the other items on your 'To Do' list until the preceding ones have been accomplished. Compare the time you took on the task to the time you allocated. This will help you to be more accurate when preparing your next and subsequent 'To Do' lists.

A common trait amongst top entrepreneurs is that they regularly use a 'To Do' list

A basic principle of effective time management is concentration of effort or focused attention. If you are able to concentrate your attention on one goal at a time, you will achieve far more than you ever will by dissipating your efforts, in trying to achieve several goals simultaneously. Many time management difficulties arise simply because we try to do too many things at once. We must realise that by prioritising our activities and tackling the most important one first, we are making the best use of our time.

Once you have developed the habit of prioritising your activities, and adhering to that list on a daily basis, you are ready for the next step, which is to set deadlines for each of the six activities. This does require a certain amount of thinking through, or planning of the content of each task. But practice at this will invariably improve your productivity by ensuring that you do not have too many activities scheduled for the next day. The mere fact that you have placed a deadline on a particular activity, puts you under a certain amount of pressure, admittedly self-imposed, but this will help you to keep at the task without distraction until it has been completed. If you do not set deadlines, you will find that Parkinson's Law comes into play, which states that: 'Work expands to fill the time available for it's completion'. When setting deadlines try, wherever possible, to meet them. If you have to extend them initially, then allow more time when setting subsequent deadlines. Avoid the trap of continually extending these deadlines as they then become meaningless and lose their effectiveness.

Delegation

In business situations, if you are in a managerial position, with staff working for you, you are often ideally placed to have more time available for planning and controlling activities, by delegating some of the tasks which you are presently performing yourself. Many managers feel they need to keep doing certain activities themselves, as that is the only way they can be certain that they will be done correctly. This is really counter-productive in the long run for two reasons. Firstly, the manager's subordinates are never going to learn how to accomplish the job and secondly, that manager is not going to grow within the organisation, but will remain at the same level performing those same activities continuously.

The key to effective delegation is to have trust in your subordinates – sufficient trust to give them the authority and responsibility to carry out the tasks which you have delegated to them. Sure, mistakes may well be made initially – this is part of the learning experience. They are only human and all humans make mistakes. However, by correct training and guidance from the manager concerned, those mistakes can be minimised, and turned into growth opportunities for both the individual and the department as a whole.

By training subordinates to do increasingly more complex tasks, and then by delegating to them tasks which you, as the manager were carrying out, you are freeing yourself to plan for expansion of your department's and hence your company's business.

One of the questions to ask yourself when listing the activities that you perform regularly is: 'Is this activity moving me closer to one of my major goals?' If the answer is: 'No', then that activity should either be delegated to someone else or eliminated altogether.

Whenever you delegate tasks to subordinates, always set a deadline for the task's completion, and ensure that your subordinate is aware of it. It is then your

Key Question

responsibility to follow-up on any task delegated, so that your subordinates know that the deadline is viewed seriously by you. This type of follow-up action will ensure that the tasks you delegate are the ones which are carried out first. If you delegate tasks without deadlines, or specify them but fail to follow-up on them, you will soon find that your subordinates will treat them light-heartedly.

Key Learning Point

To maximise your effectiveness, you should be spending most of your time (certainly 80 per cent or more) on those activities which result in the greatest return to you or your company and which you are uniquely equipped to perform by virtue of your outstanding strengths. All other activities should be delegated – ideally to colleagues or subordinates who have outstanding strengths in those areas.

Key Management Concept

The Pareto Principle or 80/20 rule

When considering what tasks to delegate to others, keep in mind the 80/20 rule, also referred to as the 'Pareto Principle'. This states that, generally, 80 per cent of the value comes from 20 per cent of your activities. Similarly, 20 per cent of the value comes from 80 per cent of your activities. It is therefore highly beneficial for your future productivity, to analyse the activities you are performing right now, and break them into those which give the greatest value. Once you have isolated the 20 per cent of high value producing activities, then you can look at the remaining 80 per cent and determine to whom they could be delegated, or whether some of them could be eliminated altogether without any detrimental consequences. Simply ask yourself: 'What would be the worst result if this activity was not performed?' If you can live with the consequences then why not spend the time you would otherwise have allocated to it, on a high value producing task? It is essential to your effectiveness, that you keep reminding yourself not to become involved in the low value activities but rather concentrate on the 20 per cent of high value ones.

Key Question

Important versus urgent activities

To use your time more effectively, you will have to differentiate between important and urgent activities. This is a major failing of most people; they rush around trying to 'put out fires' on a daily basis. Their focus of attention is on the urgent items, often at the expense of other, more important, ones. Important items may not necessarily be urgent, right at the moment, but the preparatory ground work for them should be accomplished if they are of value to you or your company. For example, you may be tasked with compiling a report on your department's projected growth over the next three years and be required to present this report to the board of directors in a month's time. Whilst there is no immediate urgency, from a time point of view, there is nevertheless a real need to commence work on it now as the content of the report and the effectiveness of your presentation are of vital importance to your department's (and possibly the entire company's) future.

When distinguishing between urgent and important activities remember that *'urgent' is time based* and *'important' is value based*. Ask yourself what return you expect from your investment in time -that is the value to be derived if and when the task is successfully accomplished. Does the expected return justify the investment in time now? If so, it is certainly important enough to rank as a top priority consideration.

When categorising activities into important and urgent, there is a tendency to believe that it is better to do something which will only take a little time and that is urgent, rather than spend five or ten minutes on an important task, which is not due for another few weeks, similar to the example outlined above. But of course this is not the case. It is far better to make a start on that important task, even though it only needs to be completed in a few weeks time, by outlining a framework, listing sources of information which you will consult, or jotting down names of people to speak to about the project. At the very least you are beginning to create the momentum so essential to becoming fully involved in that important activity. You can actually work out how long you believe the whole task is likely to take you, and then compare that with the time you have available, so as to schedule time to work on that important task.

How do you determine whether one task is more important than another? Simply by focusing on your prioritised objectives and then deciding which activity is likely to move you closest to their achievement. This will be your highest value producing activity and consequently your most important one, irrespective of its urgency.

Key Learning Point

Your prioritised objectives determine the importance of your daily activities

A point to remember when tackling one of your important tasks, is your attitude towards it. If it is a difficult task which you believe you may not finish, then obviously you will be most reluctant to start it. However, this is purely an attitude, and remember attitudes can and must be changed where they are inhibiting effective behaviour. You do not know for certain how difficult the task is, if you have not done it before. Therefore, why not assume that the task will be easy and adopt the attitude that whatever obstacles may arise, they will be overcome as you progress. Adopting a positive attitude to situations such as this, can mean the difference between, on the one hand, enjoying enormous satisfaction on the successful completion of the task or, on the other hand, the dissatisfaction of merely going through the motions of the task only to discover that the end result is nowhere near as good as it could, and should, have been had your mind and attitude been applied correctly.

You may find yourself in positions at work where you are not entirely enjoying the job which you are doing. You may therefore subconsciously be far more concerned with relatively unimportant activities rather than achieving objectives. People often do this in their personal lives as well. They are frustrated, as they know that they have the capabilities to make a far greater success of life than they have done up to now. They try to rationalise this lack of progress, by staying busy, rather than being goal orientated. This is an absolute waste of time. Keeping busy is not a worthwhile goal.

The activities in which you are regularly engaged must lead to the attainment of your goals

Key Management Concept

In Edwin C. Bliss's book *Getting Things Done,* he states: 'Everything that is accomplished in the world is the result of someone's realisation that today is the only time to act'. That is so true. The past is history. The future is uncertain, but it is where we are going to have to live. Consequently, planning for the future is essential. However, living can only be done right now, and by adopting the attitude of doing your best in the present moment, in whatever activity you happen to be performing, you will be contributing towards the most effective use of your time, as well as your own personal growth.

Autogenic conditioning

Guide to Best Practice

Do you take time out for creative thinking? It's amazing the number of large companies who employ highly qualified people for their potential intellectual contribution to the future of the organisation yet never afford them the time or opportunity to think creatively during their working hours. All managers involved in planning the policy of their company, and their personal lives of course, should take time out on a daily basis to involve themselves in some form of creative thinking, ideally autogenic conditioning. This is the best way to clarify and broaden the vision of a company or an individual. You should be in a position at work, where your secretary can hold all your calls and can keep your door closed, or better still locked, for about 40 minutes at a certain time everyday. You then let it be known that this is the time that you do not wish to be disturbed. You can then engage in autogenic conditioning and start exercising your mind. (Refer to the section on Autogenic Conditioning in Chapter 1). If it is a large company, then of course you can focus on your particular responsibilities and the objectives towards which you are committed in your division of the company. If this is not possible for you to do at work, then certainly you should embark on this quiet period everyday at home, by focusing on your personal and business goals.

Guide to Best Practice

Interruptions

People will often intrude on your time. To goal orientated achievers, like you, this should be seen as a serious criminal act. They are, in effect stealing your most precious commodity – time. These people are literally 'thieves', and you are abetting them if you do not stop them. This does not mean that you have to become rude or antisocial. People need to interrupt you occasionally, when they have genuine queries to put to you. However, once you become firm about the protection of your time, you will earn the respect of those around you and, in turn, they will come to realise the high value of time to themselves. You can minimise interruptions to your daily routine by scheduling appointments to see other people and by requesting members of your staff to consolidate the matters which they wish to discuss with you, so that these can all be raised at the same meeting.

- When working on important reports or when you require privacy to concentrate on the task at hand, close your door and make sure that people know that you do not wish to be disturbed for the next hour or so.

- Interruptions can also occur by the constant ringing of your telephone. In this regard, try to introduce a system where all calls are screened and can be transferred to other staff members who are more directly involved in answering those queries. Minimise social calls during work time, as this tends to interrupt your train of thought, as well as wasting valuable productive time.

- Plan your own calls. Set aside a certain period during the day for accepting and making calls. Important in this regard, is not to concern yourself about offending people. After a while they will come to respect your wishes and adopt the same measures themselves, especially when they see how much more productive they can become.

Procrastination

One of the biggest obstacles to effective time management is procrastination. This is, in effect, a habit. The good news is that, like any other bad habit, it can be broken with the correct use of will power, imagination, emotion and certain conditioning techniques. When you procrastinate, you tend to put off doing what has to be done, either because the task itself is perceived as being unpleasant, or a little difficult, or it may be because you do not have sufficient facts to make a decision at that time.

In this latter case, you must bear in mind, that it is a natural tendency to put off making decisions, until you have all the facts available. This is an ideal situation, which very rarely occurs, and in most cases, you will have to make decisions based on the available facts.

Making decisions quickly and changing them rarely, are hallmarks of successful people

There are several ways of overcoming procrastination. If the cause is due to your perception of the tasks as being unpleasant or uninteresting, then you should attempt doing those first. Or you can delegate them to a subordinate, who may not perceive them as being quite as unpleasant or as uninteresting as you do, provided of course, that he or she has proven to be competent in accomplishing similar tasks in the past. You can also break down unpleasant or difficult tasks into smaller, more manageable pieces. You should set deadlines in writing and build in rewards for yourself on successful completion of these tasks.

You can also begin programming yourself to 'Do It Now' as this creates a momentum of goal orientated action. You will recall learning at school one of Newton's laws, which states: 'A body at rest will remain at rest, unless acted upon by an outside force'. This law applies equally to ourselves, and we often need to apply that 'outside force' in the form of pain or pleasure associations to inaction and action respectively to create the necessary momentum. (The pain and pleasure principle will be discussed in much greater depth in Chapter 6: 'Self-motivation'.)

Another highly effective way of overcoming procrastination is by using the 'Next Step' technique. This involves consulting your plan of action and determining the next action step to be taken towards your goal. This is the one that you need to concentrate upon, even if it means spending just five minutes on it. Once you commit yourself to spending some time, (even five minutes), on it, you will quickly develop interest in what you are doing and will find that the momentum starts to build up.

Although you may only have planned to spend five minutes on the activity, once the interest is there, you are most likely to continue until that action step has been completed.

Remember that in determining the action steps that you need to take to attain your goals, you need to work from the end result. In other words the vision of that goal having already been achieved. Ask yourself: 'What is my desired end result?' Then ask: 'What needs to be done for this result to be achieved?' The answer to this latter question will determine the action steps to be taken.

Time management tips

Here are some tips to employ, to improve your time management.

Punctuality

Try to be between ten and fifteen minutes early for every appointment to allow for any possible delays such as detours or traffic jams. This gives you a better chance of being on time. Punctuality builds both self-confidence within you, and shows respect for the person you are meeting. You will also find if you arrive at your appointed destination 15 minutes ahead of schedule, it gives you sufficient time to prepare for the appointment and consequently, improves your chances of creating a more favourable impression or achieving the desired result from the meeting. You will have the opportunity of mentally rehearsing (previewing) the meeting and focusing on the desired outcome so that you are in a much better frame of mind, more self-assured and therefore able to make your presentation in a fully confident manner.

Punctuality builds both self-confidence and shows respect for the person you are meeting

Filing system

Ensure you have an effective filing system. This sounds extremely simple and of course it is, but it does avoid unnecessary wastage of time when you can put your hands on exactly what you want, when you want it. Remember the old saying: 'A place for everything, and everything in its place'. This should apply right down to items of common usage like, pencils, erasers, paper clips, and so on.

Time for creative visualisation

Determine your most creative period of the day. This is an extremely important time management principle. If you find that you are most creative during the first hour of your working day for example, you do not necessarily want to spend that time opening mail or making routine phone calls. Rather, this time should be spent in visualising and planning the future goals for your company, by using the technique of autogenic conditioning.

Correspondence

This is another area where a lot of time is wasted. Try to handle correspondence only once. When opening mail, make notes as you read, so that you do not have to re-read, and therefore spend unnecessary additional time on the same document. By making brief notes or dictating replies to the mail, as it comes in, you will find that you have more time for other activities.

Try to handle correspondence only once

3-drawer desk

Your desk should have at least three drawers in which to place incoming correspondence or documentation. In the top drawer, you should place those items which are of high value importance to the company (the ones rated 'A' on your 'To Do' list), and which require your personal attention. Try to keep a prioritised list on top of them in your drawer, so that all incoming high value items can be inserted in order of importance. Your list should be annotated accordingly. In the second drawer you would place those items of lesser importance, which could possibly be delegated to subordinates or could be handled by yourself at a later stage. These are the activities rated 'B' on your 'To Do' list. In the third drawer, place those items of apparently little importance, those rated 'C' on your 'To Do' list and include all brochures, circulars, pamphlets and general 'junk mail' that you have not already consigned to the waste paper basket. It is then a good idea to spend 15 to 20 minutes on a Friday afternoon, going through that bottom drawer, and transferring whatever items you feel will require action to the second or even the first drawer, if they have assumed greater importance during the course of that week. However, you will find that most of the items in that third drawer can be transferred directly into the waste paper basket.

Uncluttered desk

The top of your desk should be kept uncluttered. Ensure that only the papers relating to item A1 on your 'To Do' list for the day, are the ones on your desk. Everything else should be in drawers numbers one, two or three. Dispense with an 'in-tray', or basket on your desk as they only serve to remind you of the amount of work still to be done which distracts you from fully concentrating on the task at hand. Place all incoming work in one of the three drawers. Similarly, avoid having an 'out-tray' on your desk. When you have completed a task, hand it to your secretary or whoever is responsible for its further progress. It should not be within view when you tackle your next task.

Reports

You may be in a business where numerous reports are being churned out. Are the **monthly** reports absolutely essential? Could they not be transformed into **quarterly** reports? The same applies to **weekly** reports. Could they not be changed into **monthly** reports? The periodicity of these reports may be a legacy of previous years when it was necessary to have more frequent meetings.

Speed reading

Another useful time management tip is to always read with a pencil or pen in your hand. You then use it to underline or tick in the margin, any important points which you wish to refer to later, as well as using it as a pacer. Our western education system has taught us to verbalise every word that we read. That is how we have been conditioned and results in us reading at a much slower rate than that of which we are capable. Additionally, slow reading does not stimulate your brain's comprehensive ability. By pacing yourself with a pen or pencil, your reading speed will increase markedly, and your level of comprehension will simultaneously rise, because your brain is no longer bored or tending to wander off onto other subjects. Your eyes, in time, will widen their span of focus and after a lot of practice with this, you will be able to read much quicker, (up to seven times quicker in fact) and read newspapers vertically by moving your finger down the column. (The average reading speed of most people is 250 words per minute. Just by using a pencil or your finger as a pacer, you will quickly double this speed.)

Increasing your reading speed results in a simultaneous improvement in your comprehension level

Meetings

The correct handling of meetings can result in avoiding considerable time wastage as well as more effective action from the participants. Firstly, when providing notice of a meeting, an agenda should be included, together with any supporting information, providing some background to the topics and an indication of who is expected to contribute to those topics. The completion time as well as the starting time should be entered on the notice of the meeting and the agenda should include the time allocated to each topic. This very rarely happens in companies, but where it is subsequently introduced it results in far more effective meetings. Entering the completion time of the meeting on the notice assists the people attending the meeting to plan their time afterwards. If they are not aware of the scheduled completion time, they cannot plan anything thereafter, and are consequently not in a position to effectively manage their time.

The completion time as well as the starting time should be entered on the notice of the meeting and the agenda should include the time allocated to each topic

Every meeting should be followed up with minutes, which include an action and a deadline column. At the meeting, the decisions that are taken should be recorded, and whoever is responsible for taking action on those decisions, should be listed in the minutes under the 'Action By' column, and the deadline date for completion of that action should also be recorded.

Visiting colleagues/subordinates

A useful practice to adopt within your company is, instead of calling colleagues or subordinates to your office, to visit them in theirs as you are then in control of the length of the visit. Of course, it is wise to let them know beforehand that you are coming so that they can have the necessary information readily available to discuss. You can also discourage drop-in visitors, by insisting on only seeing people who have made an appointment.

Telephone conversations

In telephone conversations much time is wasted by long winded callers. One way around this is to answer your telephone with 'Hello, this is (your name) – how may I help you?' This then encourages your caller to get down to specifics right away. In cutting short someone who is protracting a call unnecessarily, add: 'Just one more thing before we hang up', or you could say: 'Right – let me see if I have those points clear in my own mind'; then you can briefly summarise the points covered and end the conversation there and then. If all else fails and you have a particularly long winded caller, knock on your desk and say: 'Sorry I have to go now – someone has just arrived!'

Television

One of the biggest time wasters is watching television. Probably 90 to 95 per cent of all television programmes have no relevance to your goals whatsoever. They are effectively robbing you of time which could be spent more productively. Once you become selective about your TV viewing, you will be reinforcing the habit that you are progressively acquiring, of taking control of your life.

Physical exercise

When planning your time usage during the day, you should include some time for physical exercise. If you can find the time to sit down and watch television and yet not find time to do some form of physical activity, then you are misusing your time. You will find that once you embark on a physical exercise programme for just half an hour each day, you will discover new sources of energy that you did not know you possessed. As a result you will be able to accomplish much more than you previously were, in the time available.

Cassette tape learning

These days most cars are fitted with cassette tape players, and the average commuter spends at least one hour per day driving to and from their place of work or between appointments. This time should be utilised effectively by the use of cassette tape playing. If you are spending up to one hour per day in your car, just imagine how this time could be put to good use by listening to positive motivational tapes or recordings concerning your particular vocation. If you are studying for a degree or diploma then record your summaries and activities and play them in the car. Record important articles to repeatedly play back to yourself for greater understanding. Use your car as your own personal mobile university.

Put these time management tips to good use – starting NOW!

The P.A.L. Life Control Process

Activity

If you are an independent businessman or woman who is in control of your time and efforts and consequently your income level, you will become a far more effective entrepreneur by introducing the P.A.L. Life Control Process into your working routine.

The P.A.L. Life Control Process involves dividing your time into Planning, Action and Leisure days. The ideal to work towards is to have every Planning, Action or Leisure day focused on the appropriate activities for a 24 hour period. Obviously, the implementation of this may not be immediately possible and you may decide to have half-days during which one half is devoted to Planning and the other half to Leisure or other combinations of the three alternatives.

A Planning day is devoted to those activities that revolve around the planning and preparation of both your Action and Leisure days. It includes all the administrative processes necessary for the consolidation of your main Action day activities which have not yet been or cannot be delegated to your support system. Your Planning days will become progressively less as your competence at the planning process increases and they can then be transformed into Leisure days (preferably) or Action days.

Action days are concentrated (at least 80 per cent of the day) on those few key activities that produce maximum value to yourself and your company. They are also the activities at which you have proven to have outstanding strengths. Initially, you should conduct an exercise to determine the activities at which you are best suited. The three or four of these activities which contribute most to the success of the company should then be focused upon and all other peripheral activities in which you are currently engaged should be delegated to your support system. If this is not immediately possible, plans should be made to either recruit additional personnel or to train existing staff to perform these activities. Your organisation will be most effective when everyone in the company is working on those key activities which best align with their outstanding strengths.

Leisure days are completely free of any activities related to Action or Planning days. They are spent with the family or on playing sport, engaging in hobbies, or outside interests and should be built in regularly to your schedule to ensure sufficient relaxation and rejuvenation so that you are at your most creative and productive when engaged on Planning and Action days.

It might sound somewhat paradoxical to suggest to a top achiever that he or she will become far more effective by taking more Leisure days. The thinking has traditionally been that, to achieve greater rewards, more time has to be spent at work and more effort put into that time. This is completely fallacious. In fact, it has been shown in numerous cases that working longer hours and working harder during those hours leads inevitably to a marked deterioration in effectiveness rather than any significant improvement. On the contrary, building in Leisure days allows the natural rejuvenation process to occur and entrepreneurs, who have adopted the P.A.L. process, find that they are able to produce twice as much productivity in half the time thereby making themselves at least four times as effective as they were previously.

The P.A.L. process should be introduced over a 90 day period. Every three months, the entrepreneur reviews his or her planned schedule of Leisure days, Action days and Planning days to implement the plans for goals to be achieved within the next 90 day period. Once this 90 day review and re-direction process becomes a habit, quantum leaps in effectiveness and results are achieved. If you are fortunate enough to be an independent businessman or woman who is in control of your time, you should introduce the P.A.L. Life Control Process into your working routine as soon as possible. You will notice enormous benefits in a very short space of time.

Summary

Key Learning Points

1. Time is a resource but unlike other resources it cannot be saved, borrowed or exchanged. It can only be spent.

2. 'Making the right choices about how you use your time is more important than doing efficiently whatever job happens to be around.' Alan Lakein.

3. Do not confuse activity with accomplishment. You may well be very busy but are you achieving your objectives?

4. Compile a daily 'To Do' list with the six most important activities for that day ranked in order of importance, with set deadlines for each activity. You are making the best use of your time when you prioritise your activities and tackle the most important one first.

5. If you are a manager, develop the habit of delegating tasks to your subordinates to ensure more time is available for your management functions. Always give your subordinates the authority as well as the responsibility to carry out delegated tasks.

6. Avoid falling into the trap of performing urgent activities at the expense of other more important ones. Remember that urgency is time based

whilst importance is value based. Your focus of attention should always be on the high value producing activities.

7. 'Everything that is accomplished in the world is the result of someone's realisation that today is the only time to act': Edwin C. Bliss. By ensuring that you optimise your actions right now, you will be contributing towards the most effective use of your time as well as your own personal growth.

8. You should engage in daily creative thinking time. (I suggest 40 minutes of autogenic conditioning.) This is the best way to clarify and broaden your vision of your personal and business goals.

9. Regard people who regularly interrupt you as thieves. They are stealing your time and, indirectly, your money. Minimise interruptions by scheduling appointments, setting aside certain times for making and receiving telephone calls, closing your door and having messages taken when working on important reports, reducing social calls during working hours and respecting the value of other people's time.

10. One of the biggest obstacles to effective time management is procrastination. You can overcome this by doing unpleasant or uninteresting tasks first or delegating them to subordinates competent to handle them, breaking down unpleasant tasks into smaller more manageable pieces, setting yourself challenging deadlines and building in rewards on completion, programming yourself to 'Do It Now', using the 'Next Step' technique and finally utilising the pain/pleasure principle by associating pleasure with the end result and pain to not taking the action steps planned.

11. Make it a habit to be at least ten to fifteen minutes early for every appointment.

12. Ensure you have an effective filing system where you can put your hands on exactly what it is you want when needed.

13. Determine your most creative period of the day and embark on autogenic conditioning for 40 minutes during this period.

14. Try to handle correspondence only once.

15. Have a three-drawer desk and place incoming correspondence or documentation into one of the three drawers, the top one being the most important, the second drawer items of lesser importance and the third drawer being those of apparently little importance.

16. Have an uncluttered desk. Do away with any 'in-trays' or 'in-baskets' utilising the three drawer system instead.

17. Is the present time stipulation on reports absolutely vital? Could monthly reports be changed to quarterly reports without any loss of effectiveness?

18. Develop the habit of speed reading utilising a pen or pencil as a pacer and marker.

19. When arranging meetings, ensure the notice includes the scheduled completion time as well as the starting time. The agenda should list the topics to be discussed, the time allocated per topic and who is expected to contribute. Additionally, any relevant supporting information which the contributors might need to have in their preparation for the meeting should be included with the notice and agenda. Follow up every meeting with minutes which include an action and a deadline column.

20. Visit colleagues in their offices rather than have them coming to yours. This way you control the length of the visit.

21. Cut out time wasting by long-winded telephone callers by using language designed to get them down to specifics right away or to summarise the points raised very quickly.

22. Become selective about your television viewing. Find out where the 'Off' button is on your television set – then use it!

23. Include some time (every day if possible) for physical exercise. Physical fitness will enable you to accomplish much more than previously in the time available.

24. Use the time spent in your car more productively by listening to cassette tapes on personal development, your particular vocation, or your own recordings of summaries of information required for degrees and diplomas.

25. If you are an independent businessman or woman (entrepreneur) who is in control of his/her time, you will maximise your effectiveness by introducing the P.A.L. (Planning, Action, Leisure) Life Control Process into your working routine.

If this is your first reading, please proceed to Chapter 5. If this is your second or subsequent reading, please carry out Activities 13, 14, 15, 16, 17, 18, 19 and 20.

Activity

Activity No. 13

Time management questionnaire

Answer the questionnaire as quickly as you can. Your first answer that springs to mind is usually the most accurate so try not to dwell on any single question. You should attempt to finish answering all 50 questions in about three minutes at the most. Check your evaluation and then, if necessary, refer again to the Time Management Tips outlined in Chapter 4.

	Yes	Sometimes	No

1. Do you compile written daily 'To Do' lists?

2. Do you prioritise your 'To Do' lists in order of importance?

3. Do you complete all items on your daily 'To Do' lists?

4. Do you set yourself weekly objectives?

5. Do you set deadlines for your activities?

6. Do you easily delegate tasks to your subordinates?

7. Do you train your subordinates to handle delegated tasks?

8. Do all the activities you perform take you closer to one of your major goals?

9. Do you set deadlines for delegated tasks?

10. Do you follow-up to ensure delegated tasks are completed by the set deadlines?

11. Do you know which of your activities are the high value producing ones?

12. Do you differentiate between important and urgent activities?

13. Do you concentrate your attention on the important rather than the urgent tasks?

14. When tackling a new task, do you assume that it will be easy and that whatever obstacles arise will be overcome as you progress?

	Yes	Sometimes	No
15. Do you believe that today is the only time to act?			
16. Do you consistently adopt the attitude of doing your best in the present moment?			
17. Do you take time out daily for creative thinking?			
18. Do you take action to minimise interruptions or intrusions on your time?			
19. Are you able to ensure uninterrupted periods for planning, report writing etc.?			
20. Do you consciously avoid making social telephone calls during office hours?			
21. Do you make decisions quickly and change them rarely?			
22. Do you easily overcome procrastination?			
23. Are you always aware of your next action step to be taken towards your major goal(s)?			
24. Do you try to be ten to fifteen minutes early for all appointments?			
25. Do you have an effective filing system? (Can you find what you are looking for without delay?)			
26. Are you aware of and do you make use of your most creative period of the day?			
27. Do you generally handle correspondence once only?			
28. Is your desk top generally uncluttered?			

	Yes	Sometimes	No

29. Do you avoid having an 'IN-TRAY' and 'OUT-TRAY' on your desk?

30. Do you use a pen, pencil or your finger as a 'pacer' when reading?

31. When organising meetings, do you advise attendees of the completion as well as the starting times?

32. Do the minutes of your meetings include 'Action By' and 'Deadline' columns?

33. Do you make a practice of visiting people in their offices rather than inviting them to your office?

34. Do you insist on appointments for people wishing to see you?

35. Do you take measures to prevent telephone interruptions when interviewing?

36. Are you able to effectively handle long-winded callers?

37. Are you selective about and able to control your TV viewing?

38. Do you schedule time for physical exercise at least four times per week?

39. Do you effectively use the time spent in your car by cassette tape learning?

40. Are you able to relax in your free time without worrying about your work?

	Yes	Sometimes	No
41. Do people know the best times to reach you?			
42. Can someone else undertake your activities if you are not available?			
43. Do you start and finish projects on time?			
44. During the past year, have you recorded how you spend your time for at least a week?			
45. Are you able to keep up with all your reading?			
46. Do you avoid taking work home or staying late at the office to finish it?			
47. Are you aware of and take steps to avoid time wasting activities?			
48. Do you avoid becoming involved in other people's work – doing things that they could or should be doing themselves?			
49. Do you take steps to reduce either the amount of paperwork or the time spent on it?			
50. Do you believe that you have sufficient time available to spend on yourself, your family, community affairs and recreational activities?			

Evaluation

Score 2 points for every 'Yes' you checked, 1 point for every 'Sometimes' and 0 points for every NO.

Then total your points and see where you fit in on the scale:

81 – 100	You manage your time very well and are in control of most situations.
61 – 80	You manage your time well some of the time. You need to be more consistent with the time saving strategies you are already using.
41 – 60	You are slipping. Don't let circumstances get the best of you. Apply more of the Time Management Tips in Chapter 4.
21 – 40	You are losing control. You are probably too disorganised to enjoy any quality time. Implement the Time Management Tips in Chapter 4 right away.
0 – 20	You are overwhelmed, scattered, frustrated and most likely under a lot of stress. Immediately put into practice the Time Management Tips in Chapter 4 and review them weekly until you have developed the habit of effective time management.

Activity

Time log of activities

Use the sheet provided as a template (to produce one for each day of the week) to record your activities in 30 minute sections. This is not to suggest that you should stop whatever you are doing every half-hour to record them but rather take the time to do so at mid-morning, lunch-time, mid-afternoon and on completion of your evening's activities. (Don't forget to include all interruptions and any unscheduled arisings.)

After one week, analyse your time spent by entering on the 'PRIORITY' column the degree of importance in value terms of each activity. (Remember the 80/20 rule – you need to identify the 20 per cent of activities that result in 80 per cent of value to you or your company. See Activity No. 15). Activity No. 16 requires you to differentiate between the importance and urgency of your activities. The degree of importance will be reflected alphabetically, the most valuable activities having an A next to them and the least valuable a C. Then the level of urgency can be shown numerically, the most urgent activities having a 1 and the least urgent a 3 next to them. Every activity should then have an alphabetical and numerical code. Naturally, the activities coded A1 are the ones that should be receiving most of your attention, followed by A2 and A3 before considering B1, B2 and B3 and so on. Place the alpha-numerical codes in the Priority column.

Daily time record: Day: Date:

Time	Activity	Priority
0600 – 0630		
0630 – 0700		
0700 – 0730		
0730 – 0800		
0800 – 0830		
0830 – 0900		
0900 – 0930		
0930 – 1000		
1000 – 1030		
1030 – 1100		
1100 – 1130		
1130 – 1200		
1200 – 1230		
1230 – 1300		
1300 – 1330		
1330 – 1400		
1400 – 1430		
1430 – 1500		
1500 – 1530		
1530 – 1600		
1600 – 1630		
1630 – 1700		
1700 – 1730		
1730 – 1800		
1800 – 1830		
1830 – 1900		
1900 – 1930		
1930 – 2000		
2000 – 2030		
2030 – 2100		
2100 – 2130		
2130 – 2200		

Please reproduce seven of these sheets, one for every day of the week.

Activity No. 15

Applying the 80/20 rule

In carrying out Activity No. 14, you identified over the course of the week the activities which you regularly performed and you coded them on a priority basis. You now need to focus on those activities which bring you and your company the greatest value. Following the 80/20 rule you should find that the 20 per cent of activities producing 80 per cent of value are those you have coded A1, A2 and A3. Your task in this activity is to re-schedule your activities (and delegate others) in order to ensure that your time is being spent most advantageously. If you have accurate, clearly defined objectives then knowing what activities to concentrate on yourself, what to delegate, and what to eliminate completely will be a simple exercise.

Use the 'To Do' list (see Activity No. 18) and list the activities that you will personally be performing to achieve your top priority objectives, Then use the Delegation Check list (see Activity No. 20) and delegate activities with deadlines for each one to those subordinates who have proved capable of completing those tasks in the past.

Activity No. 16

Activity

Differentiating between important and urgent activities

Using the activity priority grid overleaf and the list of activities regularly performed, which were identified on Activity No. 14, place all the activities into their appropriate box based on their degree of importance and urgency. The most important activities, those with the highest value to you/your company, would appear in row A and the least in row C. The most urgent activities would appear in column 1 and the least in column 3.

Using abbreviations, (e.g. A for appointments, M for meetings, R for reports, T for telephone calls, etc.) enter your identified activities into the grid, to see whether the bulk of your time is being consumed by important or urgent activities.

Activity priority grid

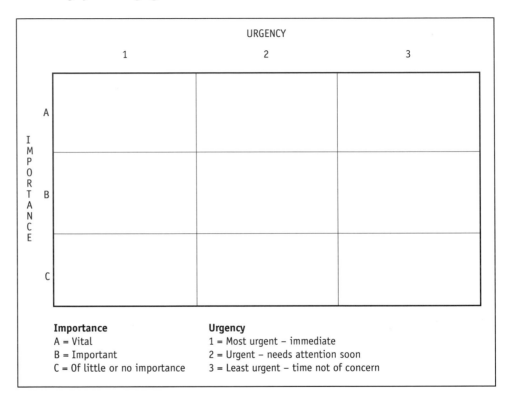

Importance
A = Vital
B = Important
C = Of little or no importance

Urgency
1 = Most urgent – immediate
2 = Urgent – needs attention soon
3 = Least urgent – time not of concern

Activity No. 17

Assessing your time utilisation

List below the most frequent and time consuming urgent activities you usually perform. To the right of each activity, state the degree of importance. Then compare the list with activities allocated to the grid in Activity No. 16. You should now ensure that your daily 'To Do' list (Activity No. 18) focuses on those activities shown in column A below.

Current urgent activities	Degree of importance		
	A	B	C

Code: A = Vital   B = Important   C = Of little or no importance

Activity No. 18

Compilation of your daily 'To Do' list

Ideally, you should be using a two page-per-day diary with a list of activities to be performed as well as scheduled appointments and events on the left hand page and a record of daily happenings on the right hand page. However, if you are not using this type of diary, you can compile your own daily 'To Do' list by using the following pages.

List the activities to be performed the next day. Then prioritise them by asking yourself 'Which activity will move me closer to my major goal?' Cognisance will also have to be taken, of course, of the order in which activities need to be performed when determining priorities.

As each activity is completed tick the check/transfer column. Where an activity cannot be finalised and further action is needed, transfer it to another date and annotate the check column with a T and the date. So, for example, an activity which you were re-scheduling for 25th April would be annotated T25/4 in the check or transfer column.

Daily 'To Do' list (record daily happenings overleaf)

Day:

Date:

Priority	Check or Transfer	Activity	Appointments/Events	Time

Record of daily happenings

Day: Date:

Time	Record of happenings or services provided	Hrs	Min

Activity

Activity No. 19

Assessing your urgent activities

Urgent activities that are not really important or could be handled by someone else obstruct your important tasks. List below the most frequent and time consuming urgencies you usually face. To the right of each activity, under the heading of 'future action', state whether that particular urgent activity is important, who can best deal with it and what you can do to prevent it from using up your time if it is not an important interruption.

Urgent activity	Future action

Activity No. 20

Delegation checklist

To become truly effective at time management, you must be a proficient manager who knows how and what to delegate to his/her subordinates.

Having analysed your activities (Activities 14, 15, 16, 17 and 19) you should now have a clear idea of the activities that can be delegated to others as well as those that could be eliminated altogether without any serious adverse consequences.

Use the delegation checklist to allocate tasks to your subordinates. Remember to ensure that your subordinates are given the authority to carry out the responsibilities delegated. Be sure you follow-up on the deadlines set for completion of the delegated tasks, by diarising the deadline date.

Delegation checklist

To Whom Delegated	Date	Priority	Responsibility/Task	Check (✔) or Transfer (T)	Due Date	Diarised

How to improve your self-image and self-confidence

Your self-image is the key to your personality and behaviour and it sets the limits on what you are going to accomplish. You will never outgrow the limits which you place on your ability to get somewhere. Therefore, if you have an inadequate self-image, and do not believe that you are worthy of the goals you have set for yourself, then you are wasting your time striving for them because, as long as your subconscious mind is conditioned to believe that you do not deserve to achieve your goals, it will always find ways of inhibiting your progress. No matter how deliberate your conscious actions may be towards your goals, if, subconsciously, you have an inadequate self-image, then you will not achieve them, because you will always act, feel and perform in accordance with what you imagine to be true about yourself and your environment.

You must recognise that a defective self-image can damage the quality of your life in spite of positive self-motivation and willpower on your part. Dennis Waitley in his book: *The Psychology of Winning* hits the nail on the head when he says: 'It's not what you are that holds you back, it's what you think you are not.' That is so true. People tend to focus far too much on their 'failures' or mistakes of the past without learning from them.

Key Learning Point

You will always act, feel and perform in accordance with your self-image

'Failures' and attitude

I want, at this point, to put failures and past mistakes into their correct perspective. Every habit that you now have was acquired by you making mistakes and then correcting them. In effect, 'failure' became part of the learning process. Think back to when you were learning to drive your car, to type or even the simple act of tying a bow or a tie. You made mistakes – but you learnt from them and gradually eliminated them until you had mastered the habit. In other words, you treated this as negative feedback and changed your plan accordingly. This is important. In life, you will always have obstacles to overcome if you are to be truly successful, and these must be seen in the right light. This is how you acquire the success habit. You will make mistakes – that is inevitable, but it is the attitude which you take towards them that is so important for your self-image and your ultimate victory. If you can train yourself to accept these mistakes as the learning experiences that they truly are, then you will be using them positively to grow.

It is useful to recall that Thomas Edison failed more than 10,000 times before discovering the electric light bulb. Yet no one would ever describe him as a failure. His attitude to his mistakes was that he was merely eliminating the alternatives. How could he possibly become anything but a success with that attitude? However, if he had had an inadequate self-image, chances are he would have given up long before his 10,000 'failures'.

Research shows that in 90 per cent of cases, the cause of failure can be attributed to quitting – giving up when often success is just around the corner. Persistence is a tremendous quality to develop – an essential prerequisite to be truly successful. But it is virtually impossible to be persistent with an inadequate self-image.

In 90 per cent of cases, the cause of failure can be attributed to giving up, when often success is just around the corner

Key Learning Point

Someone once said: 'I would rather attempt something great and fail than attempt nothing at all and succeed.' Unfortunately, that does not appear to be a very widely held philosophy largely due to the fear of failure. But failure is not the worst result – not trying is. If you try, you can succeed but if you won't try you have already failed. Success doesn't mean that you can't fail but it does mean that you will not accept failure as an end result. You must continually remind yourself that no truly successful person has ever reached that level without 'failing'. In fact, they have accepted the inevitability of 'failure' as a necessary stepping stone to success. This is the attitude that you need to cultivate in developing your self-image.

Conditioning

Your self-image at the moment, that is the mental picture you hold of yourself, is a result of your past conditioning, whether this be positive or negative. And your past conditioning will largely have been due to the influences that authority-type figures such as your parents, teachers, sports coaches and the like had on your earlier belief system. You need to be aware of how important your belief system is to your performance level, as your beliefs will actually determine the amount of your potential that you will use and obviously that will have a direct bearing on the actions you take and consequently the results you achieve in life.

Key Learning Point

Your beliefs determine the amount of your potential you use

Changing your self-image

If your self-image is the result of your past experiences, positive and negative, does it mean that to change your self-image you have to subject yourself to new experiences? Fortunately not, although that, of course, would be a solution. But there is a far easier and quicker method which involves the regular and positive use of your imagination. You already know (from Chapter 2) that your subconscious mind cannot differentiate between a real experience and one that is vividly imagined. This means that you can programme your subconscious mind with pictures of yourself as the winner you are to become. Winners in life always hold in mind the self-image of the person they want to be. And then they act out that role, rather like children playing a game of 'Let's pretend'. To become a winner you have to initially act the part. You have to walk, talk, look and feel like a winner every day. That starts to build a positive self-image. You also need to be able to visualise your successes **before** they occur.

Your self-image will be influenced by the way in which you evaluate your attributes, ranging from your physical appearance through to your intellectual capabilities. For example, a 74 per cent result in an examination could have positive or negative influences on your self-image depending on your evaluation of the result. If your goal was to exceed the pass mark of 60 per cent, then the result would have a positive influence. If, on the other hand, you had set your sights on attaining a distinction (75 per cent or higher) then the result could have a negative influence on your self image – *if you allow it to*. The choice is yours.

Any permanent change in your personality or behaviour has to be preceded by a change in your self-image

Key Learning Point

Any permanent change in your personality or behaviour has to be preceded by a change in your self-image. Why do most people have an inadequate self-image? Usually, it is because of the amount of negative conditioning to which they have been subjected since birth. As babies and then as young children, they were completely dependent upon their parents or guardians. Later at school they became conformists with very little encouragement or opportunity to use their own individual initiative. They were taught to be humble, self-effacing, modest people who should make light of their strengths and emphasise their weaknesses. This is not to suggest that you should suddenly become egotistic. Far from it. However, to develop an adequate self-image requires taking an honest and objective look at your strengths and weaknesses and then using those strengths and delegating, where possible your weaknesses. Life is far too short to spend time attempting to transform weaknesses into strengths. In any event, it usually results in your becoming stronger in these weaknesses!

It is far more productive to focus on using more of your strengths. Obviously, where a weakness constitutes a major obstacle to your future progress, it requires attention but in the main, most weaknesses can and should be delegated to others with strengths in those areas.

Key Learning Point

Focus on your strengths – delegate your weaknesses

An inadequate self-image can also be the result of a traumatic or highly embarrassing experience. The solution, in these instances, is to replay the experience in your mind, but this time ensuring your actions produce a favourable outcome. By constantly replaying the 'modified' experience, your subconscious mind will soon accept it as real and mould your self-image accordingly.

Psychological research indicates that people spend approximately 70 per cent of their time talking to themselves – not audibly of course – but nevertheless sending messages through to their subconscious minds. It therefore makes sense to ensure that the messages you send to yourself should be positive, particularly when you consider the effects on your self-image.

Mention was made in the introduction to this book of the need for you to take responsibility for your own destiny in life. This is essential to building a correct self-image. It is so easy to look around and find excuses for your lack of progress. That is negative thinking and will get you nowhere. You have to take responsibility for your own progress if you are to make things happen. There will always be a plentiful share of losers who have ready-made excuses for their situations in life. But the world will always have room for the winners in life who, being goal orientated opportunity seekers, have no time for excuses.

Practical steps to improve your self-image

Action Checklist

1.   Use your strengths

Life is full of people who possess all the knowledge they will ever need to be successful, yet for one reason or another, never apply this knowledge and, consequently, never become the successes they should be. Everyone possesses the necessary qualities to attain their genuinely desired goals but, unfortunately, most do not believe this to be the case. They have more than enough strengths but choose to focus, again by virtue of the conditioning process, more on their weaknesses.

Everyone possesses the strengths needed to attain their genuinely desired goals

Key Learning Point

Once you have identified your strengths you should make a daily practice of using one or more of them. The more often you do this the greater the positive reinforcement you are feeding back to your subconscious mind. You should also work on whatever major weakness you feel may be holding back your progress towards your goals. You do this by confronting your fears head on, and putting yourself to the test in trying situations. For example, you may be shy and retiring by nature and avoid, at all costs, the prospect of stating your views on a subject publicly. In meetings, you may feel strongly about a particular point but do not voice your opinion due to some, usually subconscious, fear of having that view rejected or criticised or of looking foolish in front of others. The only way to overcome this fear is to take your courage in your hands and speak up. Do it. Your action will dispel your fear like a pin pricking a balloon. The next time a similar situation arises, you will probably still feel a little nervous, but not quite as much as the first time. After a few such occasions, you will wonder why you were so fearful initially. This will have a tremendously positive influence on your self-image and level of self-confidence.

2.   Autogenic conditioning

Top achievers regularly bring to mind the self-image of the person they are becoming. Your next step therefore is to carry out daily creative visualisation exercises in which you see yourself as the winner that you are going to become. Visualise yourself with your goals attained, enjoying the benefits and rewards of their attainment. Spend 20 minutes twice a day on these visualisation exercises utilising the autogenic conditioning technique outlined in Chapter 1. Not only must you see yourself with the goals already achieved, but you must believe you are worthy of achieving them. Like any other belief it strengthens with repetition and the daily visualisation and emotionalisation exercises together with the reading of your affirmation cards as explained in Chapter 2 will provide this repetition.

Key Learning Point

Top achievers regularly bring to mind the self-image of the person they are becoming

3.   Television viewing

The next step is to limit your television viewing to selected shows. When indiscriminate viewing becomes habitual, it starts destroying your creative ability. The imagination needs constant use to improve its creativity. In the same way that a physical muscle will atrophy if not used, so will your imagination weaken commensurate with its degree of neglect. Used correctly, television can be beneficial but does require becoming selective about what is regularly fed into your mind.

4.   Feedback

Feedback in the form of weekly reviews of successes over the past seven days serves to build up your self-image and self-confidence level. This is best achieved by keeping a diary of events which is maintained daily. Record as accurately as you can, the date and time when each individual goal set for that week was attained. It doesn't matter how small or easy the goals were that you accomplished. What does matter is that you had set targets for that week which were met. This reinforces the positive conditioning of your subconscious mind, building your success momentum in the process.

Regular feedback (weekly reminders of your successes) reinforces the positive conditioning of your subconscious mind

Key Learning Point

5. Outward appearances

The image which you project to others is influenced by a number of different factors, such as the clothes you wear, your hairstyle, the cleanliness of your shoes, the state of your garden or workshop at home, the condition of your car and so on. These are all outward manifestations of your self-image. If you take pride in your personal possessions and look after them well, then you will be far more likely to be proud of and look after your own self-image.

6. Accepting compliments

An adequate self-image means being fully satisfied and comfortable with who you are. Can you accept compliments with a smile and simply say: 'Thank you' when they are paid, or do you find yourself embarrassed and playing down your accomplishments? This latter response, whilst wrong, is completely understandable. If this is a typical reaction on your part, then you need to change it immediately as it will adversely affect your self-image. This does not mean that you need to become a braggart, always blowing your own trumpet. It simply means that whenever you are praised by anyone, graciously thank them, as your ability to accept compliments is a clear indication of someone with a satisfactory self-image.

7.   Introduce yourself

Make a point of being the first to introduce yourself in any new company, by stating your name clearly and pleasantly, offering your hand and looking the other person straight in the eyes. When answering your telephone, give your name at the outset – before you ask who is calling. This creates the impression of openness and honesty and lets the caller know that you have a lot of self respect.

8.   Physical exercise

You have to look like a winner before you become one. Regular physical exercise is essential to having a healthy body and mind. You have already been urged to relax (and visualise yourself as the winner you are to become) for at least 20 minutes twice a day. That is your mental exercise. You also need to embark on a physical exercise programme in which you engage in some vigorous physical activity for at least 35 to 45 minutes, four or more times a week. You should, of course, consult your doctor before commencing an exercise programme.

You have to look like a winner before you become one

9.   Cassette tape learning

Listening to cassette tape recordings can greatly improve your self-image and self-confidence levels, particularly if you are someone who spends a considerable amount of time in your car travelling to and from work or appointments. This point was also made when discussing how best to manage your time in Chapter 4. You do not have to be consciously concentrating on the message of the cassette tape for it to have an effect on your subconscious mind. These tapes can either be those which feature motivational speakers providing inspirational techniques on improving your self-image and self-confidence or they can be recorded by yourself with affirmations about the achiever you are becoming. You can record your goals and plans of action as well as the new empowering beliefs you wish to hold.

10. Become an optimist

Become an optimist. Associate with other optimists. It can become an extremely uplifting and stimulating experience to be in the company of people who seem to have a perpetually positive outlook on life. You will also find that most of these optimists happen to be successful and happy. These are the people that choose to look for (and find) the positive side of other people and situations; who see obstacles in their path as the challenges that they really are; who are solution rather than problem orientated; who are always first to welcome strangers and introduce them to others; who always seem to be cheerful and enjoying life; who regularly praise but never criticise or condemn other people; who do not complain about situations but positively do something about them. These are the people who are satisfied with their self-images. You know them. Become one of them – your self-image and self-confidence will benefit enormously.

11. Acting the role

Mention was made at the beginning of this chapter of the desirability of acting out the role of the person you wish to become. It is a proven fact that actors and actresses when playing roles consistently over a lengthy period (three months or more) tend to adopt the behavioural traits of the characters they are portraying. In the same way, it is suggested that you should act out regularly the role of the person you have decided to become. If you continually act as though you possess the self-image and self confidence that you are striving for, you will accelerate the development of those qualities.

You will accelerate the development of the future by acting the role now

12. Persistence

Cultivate the habit of persistence. After desire it is the most vital quality in your success make-up. Look at any successful personality and inevitably you will conclude that persistence was essential to their success. There are millions of people who have the talents, abilities, skills, qualities, education and a host of other characteristics which are considered necessary for success, but who lack the one ingredient which would ensure it – persistence. You can develop persistence by prioritising your activities and then concentrating your attention on the top priority item until it has been completed. You cannot really expect to have sustained persistence if you do not have a strong enough desire for the goal being pursued. To continuously fuel the fire of desire and ensure your motivational level is consistently high requires you to conduct autogenic conditioning sessions twice a day, 20 minutes a session.

13. Self-respect

Improve your self respect. One of the best ways of achieving this is to do things for others without expecting anything in return. Try giving anonymously. Then it is impossible for you to receive any direct return. However, the feeling of self satisfaction and the increase in self respect that acts of this nature will engender, will provide you with a far longer lasting reward – a healthy self-image. You will also find that the Law of Returns comes into operation and the more you give to others – the more you will have to give.

Key Learning Point

The more you give to others – the more you will have to give

14. Forgive yourself

Forgive yourself your mistakes. As a general rule, we tend to readily forgive others for their mistakes but do not extend that same courtesy to ourselves. Rather we berate ourselves whenever we make mistakes or 'fail' in our endeavours. If we knew the negative conditioning effects of these actions, we would understand that it is far more beneficial to the development of our self-image and self confidence to quickly forgive ourselves those mistakes realising that we are only human and that it is human nature to make mistakes occasionally. In fact, as I have mentioned earlier, no meaningful success was ever achieved without the making of mistakes at some stage of the process. Remember that making mistakes should not be seen as a criticism of yourself but of your actions at that particular time. In the same way that, when motivating other people, you would criticise the deed and not the doer, make sure that you don't hold recriminations against yourself or start accusing yourself of being a 'failure' or being deficient in any qualities necessary for attaining success. Treat all mistakes as the learning experiences which, realistically, they are.

15. Biographies

Read the biographies of successful achievers. This will inspire you to greater efforts, especially if the person you are reading about has become a winner in your particular field of interest. However, a word of warning here. Do not try to duplicate that person's methods or personal qualities – at best you will be a poor imitation. Remember to be yourself – you are unique – there is no one else in this world quite like you. You have your own array of abilities, skills, talents, qualities which, once directed, will prove to be entirely adequate to attain your goals. There is no need to try to be like someone else. By all means be inspired by the achievements of others; they should stimulate your desire and consequently increase your motivation to succeed by using what you have. Ask yourself what these successful achievers needed to believe about their own abilities to succeed as you may wish to adopt some of these beliefs yourself.

16. Perception of others

You know that your present self-image is the product of your past thinking and doing. Similarly, your self-image in the future will be the product of your thoughts and deeds from today. Give some thought as to how you would like others to perceive you and then make sure that your actions are consistent with that perception.

Key Learning Point

Your self-image in the future will be the product of your thoughts, feelings and actions from today

17. Goal orientated

Being goal orientated is essential to developing your self-image. Too many people confuse activity with accomplishment and as a goal orientated winner you must ensure your activities are leading toward the attainment of your major goals. When you have developed the habit of regularly listing the activities which will lead to the attainment of your major goals and then once they have been carried out, crossing them off as you complete them, you will be cultivating a success habit and greatly enhancing your self-image and self-confidence levels.

18. Live one day at a time

Try to live one day at a time. Alcoholics Anonymous have this as their underlying success philosophy. Once an alcoholic has admitted that he has a problem, he does not say that he will not drink in the future. However, he does make a commitment that he will not have a drink **today** and the Alcoholics Anonymous support system helps him in that goal. When the next day arrives, the same policy is adopted. This is effectively conditioning or programming a success habit. For someone like an alcoholic to contemplate the possibility of never again having another drink would be far too great a goal to set initially. However, if he can achieve the goal of abstaining for one day, that in itself is a success which goes into the subconscious mind and everyday that he does not drink thereafter increases the likelihood that he will not drink again in the future. In the same way you can build your self-image and self-confidence levels by living one day at a time. If you realise that your eventual goal is a successful life and that this is made up of successful years, months, weeks, days and that each day comprises a series of successful acts, you can then see that by concentrating your attention on doing your best in the particular act in which you are currently engaged, is inevitably leading towards a successful life.

Concentrating your attention on doing your best in the particular act in which you are currently engaged, inevitably leads towards a successful life

Key Learning Point

19. Mind control

Try keeping your mind **on** what you want and **off** what you do not want. This is much easier said than done. However, with the daily mental training (autogenic conditioning) that you will be carrying out regularly, you will soon have the control of thought which allows you to focus on what you choose and not allow negative thoughts to intrude on your positive thought pattern.

20. Fear of failure

An inhibiting factor to the development of an adequate self-image is the fear of failure and its associated anxieties or doubts about your ability to achieve. These can be overcome by the regular use of the autogenic conditioning periods where you are focusing on seeing yourself with the end result, with your goals fulfilled and the rewards and benefits resulting from those achieved goals flowing to you and your family. Additionally, worries need to be placed into their correct perspective. Earl Nightingale in his excellent cassette tape programme: *Lead The Field* states that research into worries shows that: '40 per cent never happen, 30 per cent concern past events which cannot now be changed; 12 per cent are needless worries about our health; ten per cent are petty miscellaneous worries and eight per cent are the real legitimate worries'. Consequently, 92 per cent of all worries are completely unnecessary. So the next time you catch yourself worrying about something, remind yourself of those statistics and try switching your mind on to the thoughts you want to think about.

Key Learning Point

92 per cent of all worries are completely unnecessary

Positive thoughts can be engendered by asking yourself the right questions. Remember the cause and effect relationship that exists between thoughts and conditions. If you start asking your brain the right questions, it will search and find positive answers. Develop the habit of asking yourself questions such as: 'How can I improve my service to others?' or, 'How can I use this situation to benefit myself and others?' Then your brain will search your memory bank and come up with answers to those questions. (If you catch yourself asking questions such as: 'What's wrong with my life?' or, 'Why do I always fail like this?' then you must change those questions immediately as, in the same way that your brain will search for positive answers to positive questions, it will equally search for negative answers if you ask negative questions.)

Summary

1. 'It's not what you are that holds you back, it's what you think you are not.' Dennis Waitley

2. 'Failure' is an inevitable part of the learning process.

3. Your present self-image is the result of your past conditioning. Your self-image in the future will be a result of your conditioning from now onwards.

4. You can change your self-image by replaying past negative experiences but this time with the positive outcomes you wanted. Remember, your subconscious mind cannot tell the difference between a real experience and one vividly imagined.

5. You spend approximately 70 per cent of your time sending messages through to your subconscious mind. Make sure those messages are positive empowering ones.

6. Choose to identify, through previous achievements, your strengths and then to focus upon using them. If you identify a major weakness, focus on ways of converting it into a strength or delegating it to someone with strengths in that area.

7. On a daily basis, you should be visualising and emotionalising yourself as a winner. (Autogenic conditioning twice a day for 20 minutes a session.)

8. Take charge of your television viewing habits. Become selective about the programmes you watch.

9. Review your successes weekly by recording your achievements daily in a diary or journal.

10. Take pride in your personal possessions and your outward appearance.

11. Accept compliments graciously with a simple, sincere 'Thank you'.

12. Be the first to introduce yourself in social situations or when answering the telephone.

13. Embark on a physical exercise programme involving some form of aerobic activity for at least 35 minutes, four or five times a week.

14. If you spend a substantial time in your car, use that to best effect by playing cassette tapes on personal development or recorded affirmations by yourself relating to your goals and the beliefs that you wish to hold.

15. Become a proactive optimist and associate with other goal orientated individuals.

16. Regularly act out the role of the person you have decided to become. It will greatly accelerate the development of your self-confidence and self-image.

17. Cultivate the habit of persistence by prioritising your activities and then concentrating your attention on the top priority task until it has been completed. If your persistence level is not as high as it should be, the chances are that your desire is not strong enough. In this case, use the regular autogenic conditioning sessions to increase your desire.

18. Improve your self respect by doing things for others without expecting anything in return.

19. Forgive yourself your mistakes realising that they are the learning experiences necessary for your eventual success.

20. Read the biographies of successful achievers to help inspire you to greater efforts.

21. Your self-image will be influenced by the opinions of others. The opinions of others will be influenced by your thoughts, feelings and actions. Take control of the process.

22. Become goal orientated on a daily basis. Ensure that you have set outcomes for each day and that your activities are leading towards the attainment of these outcomes.

23. Focus on making today a success and tomorrow will look after itself. Use the same philosophy that has proved so successful over the years for Alcoholics Anonymous, namely to live one day at a time.

24. Control your thinking process by focusing on what you want and not on what you do not want. Remember that the best way to stop thinking about what you **do not** want is to think about what you **do** want.

25. Overcome the fear of failure by focusing on the positive rewards of successful attainment of your goals. Recognise that failure will be inevitable if you do not take the action steps and then sense the pain that will result. This should spur you into action.

If this is your first reading of this book, please proceed to Chapter 6. If this is your second or subsequent reading, please carry out Activities 21, 22, 23, 24 and 25.

Activity

Activity No. 21

Developing self-confidence: acting the role

The development of a positive self-image and increased self confidence can be greatly accelerated by acting as though you were already that person. Consequently, over the course of the next week, you should act in all situations as though you possessed the utmost self-confidence and were a completely self assured individual with all the attributes that you associate with that person. Record the outcomes below.

Outcomes from acting the role

Day 1

Day 2

Day 3

Day 4

Day 5

Day 6

Day 7

Activity No. 22

Identifying strengths and weaknesses

To carry out this activity, cast your mind back to three notable successes in your life. These can be recent or they can go back some considerable time but they must be significant achievements which made you feel really good about yourself. Everyone has had at least three major successes in their lives that they are really proud of and you are no exception so go ahead and reflect on these achievements.

On the following pages write down your three significant achievements. For each one, record why you felt good about that particular achievement at the time and list the obstacles that you overcame in attaining your goal.

Then, on the following pages list the strengths (the qualities, abilities, skills) that you used in that successful achievement. Do not confine yourself to one or two strengths. You exhibited far more at the time and you must now attempt to recall each one of them. (Qualities such as concentration of effort, organisational skills, planning ability, self-confidence, determination, persuasive ability, sound judgement, energy, charm, tact, will power, imagination, persistence, courage, sympathy, cheerfulness and so on.) You should also list under the 'weaknesses' column the characteristics or qualities which inhibited your progress initially and which you had to overcome to succeed.

Once you have completed this exercise for all successes then you need to review the strengths that you have listed in each of those achievements. Those strengths are still with you – you still possess them even though you may not be currently utilising them. Your task therefore is to make sure that you are exercising these strengths on a regular (ideally daily) basis. Additionally, if you have identified any major weaknesses which still exist as significant obstacles in the path to your future goals, the conversion of these weaknesses into strengths should now form part of your goal setting plan of action. The emphasis, however, should be placed on using your strengths. (Too many people spend their lives focusing on their weaknesses and neglect their strengths.)

Identifying strengths and weaknesses

Achievement No. 1

Reasons for feeling good about your achievement

Obstacles overcome in attaining your goal

Achievement No. 2

Reasons for feeling good about your achievement

Obstacles overcome in attaining your goal

Achievement No. 3

Reasons for feeling good about your achievement

Obstacles overcome in attaining your goal

Strengths and weaknesses identified in achievement No.___

Strengths	Weaknesses

Use this format for the strengths and weaknesses identified in achievements 1-3.

Activity

A

Analysing your belief system

List any disempowering beliefs about your own abilities which may have inhibited your progress in the past. Alongside them, list the empowering beliefs which you now intend using to replace the previous disempowering beliefs. (Refer to the list of suggested empowering beliefs to assist you.)

List the disempowering beliefs which have held you back in the past	List the empowering beliefs which you intend using to replace the old beliefs

Empowering beliefs

- IF IT IS TO BE IT IS UP TO ME

- QUITTERS NEVER WIN – WINNERS NEVER QUIT

- PREVENTION IS BETTER THAN CURE

- THE PAST DOES NOT GOVERN THE FUTURE

- I NEVER FAIL – I LEARN

- PROBLEMS ARE MY TEACHERS

- IF YOU WANT TO SOAR WITH EAGLES – DON'T HANG AROUND WITH TURKEYS

- THE MORE I GIVE, THE MORE I HAVE TO GIVE

- WINNING STARTS WITH BEGINNING

- THIS TOO SHALL PASS

- YOU CAN IF YOU BELIEVE YOU CAN

- YOU REAP WHAT YOU SOW

- DO IT BECAUSE IT'S RIGHT – NOT EXPEDITIOUS

- I AM ALWAYS ABLE TO ACQUIRE WHATEVER MONEY I NEED FOR GOALS TO WHICH I AM TRULY COMMITTED

- I AM PREPARED TO DO WHATEVER IT TAKES TO ACHIEVE MY GOALS WITHOUT HARMING ANYONE IN THE PROCESS

- DO THE THING AND YOU'LL HAVE THE POWER

- ALL HUMAN BEINGS HAVE UNLIMITED POTENTIAL

- EVERY PERSON HAS A RESPONSIBILITY TO BE THE BEST HE CAN BE (I HAVE A RESPONSIBILITY TO BE THE BEST I CAN)

- WE ALL HAVE A RESPONSIBILITY TO MAKE THE WORLD A BETTER PLACE

- WINNERS ARE NOT BORN – THEY ARE MADE

- THE ONLY REAL LIMITATIONS ON WHAT YOU CAN ACCOMPLISH IN YOUR LIFE ARE THOSE YOU IMPOSE ON YOURSELF

- THERE CAN BE NO GREAT SUCCESS WITHOUT GREAT COMMITMENT

- YOU NEED THE SUPPORT AND CO-OPERATION OF OTHER PEOPLE TO ACHIEVE ANY WORTHWHILE GOAL

- THE REWARDS YOU RECEIVE IN LIFE COME AS A RESULT OF YOUR PERFORMANCE, NOT YOUR POTENTIAL

- IF WHAT YOU WANT IN THE FUTURE IS DIFFERENT FROM WHAT YOU'VE GOT IN THE PRESENT, YOU HAVE TO CHANGE WHAT YOU'VE BEEN DOING

- IT IS ALWAYS MORE PRODUCTIVE TO FOCUS ON WHAT YOU PERCEIVE AS CHALLENGES OR OPPORTUNITIES RATHER THAN ON WHAT YOU PERCEIVE AS PROBLEMS OR SET-BACKS; TO FOCUS ON REASONS WHY YOU CAN ACHIEVE YOUR GOAL RATHER THAN ON REASONS WHY YOU CANNOT; TO FOCUS ON SOLUTIONS RATHER THAN ON EXCUSES

- YOUR ATTITUDE TOWARDS OBSTACLES RATHER THAN THE OBSTACLES THEMSELVES WILL DETERMINE IN THE END WHETHER YOU SUCCEED OR FAIL

- THE KEY TO SUCCESS LIES IN YOUR MANNER OF THINKING – YOUR ATTITUDE – IT DETERMINES HOW YOU FEEL AND BEHAVE

- FAILURE IS A VITAL AND NECESSARY PART OF THE ACHIEVEMENT PROCESS

- FORTUNE FAVOURS THE BRAVE

- YOU LOSE WHAT YOU DO NOT USE

- IF YOU WANT TO GET THE RESULTS THAT WINNERS GET, YOU MUST FIRST THINK LIKE A WINNER THINKS

- THE DOMINANT FORCE IN YOUR EXISTENCE IS THE THINKING YOU CONSISTENTLY ENGAGE IN

- YOU ARE EMPOWERED TO CREATE YOUR OWN REALITY

- THERE IS SOME BENEFIT TO BE HAD FROM EVERY ADVERSITY

- EACH ONE OF YOUR BELIEFS IS A CHOICE

- YOU ARE NEVER DEFEATED UNTIL YOU ACCEPT DEFEAT AS A REALITY, AND DECIDE TO STOP TRYING

- YOU ALREADY POSSESS THE ABILITY TO EXCEL IN AT LEAST ONE KEY AREA OF YOUR LIFE

- ACTIONS SPEAK LOUDER THAN WORDS

- DON'T TELL THE WORLD WHAT YOU CAN DO – SHOW THEM

- DO IT RIGHT – BECAUSE IT'S RIGHT – AND DO IT RIGHT NOW

- I HAVE THE DISCIPLINE TO FOLLOW MY PLAN OF ACTION

Activity

Building your self-image

In order to boost your self-image and self-confidence levels, think of a situation which would normally fill you with fear and trepidation. It could be a public speaking engagement or contributing towards a meeting in front of many other people. It may simply be lacking self-confidence in social situations. Find out when the next similar situation or event is likely to take place. Diarise the date for you to attend. Then, set yourself a goal of doing what you fear most in that situation. For example, if it is contributing to the discussion at a public meeting, determine beforehand the point or points that you would like to convey to the meeting and then rehearse those points and, whilst carrying out your daily autogenic conditioning exercises, see yourself standing up and conveying your message in an articulate and self confident manner. Then you must follow through on this preparation. Remember, nothing ever happens without ACTION. You may have the best intentions in the world but, until these are transformed into action, nothing meaningful will change in your life.

Once you have subjected yourself to this type of situation or event once or twice, you will notice enormous gains in your self-confidence. It is a personal growth process and only you will know and relish the true benefits of that process to your self-image.

Activity No. 25

Improving your self-confidence by replaying 'failures'

Write down in detail (in the table below) whatever reasons you can think of for lacking self confidence in particular situations. Reflect on three past 'failures' and your reactions to them. Once you have identified them, you can now take steps to re-programme yourself by replaying the events in your mind, during your autogenic conditioning sessions, only this time changing the outcome to a favourable one.

Reasons for lacking self confidence in particular situations

_____

_____

_____

Three past 'failures' and your reactions to them

1

2

3

'Replayed' situations with favourable outcomes

1

2

3

Use your autogenic conditioning sessions to repeatedly replay these situations with favourable outcomes until your self-confidence has improved to a high level.

Activity No. 26

Qualities of an acknowledged achiever

Choose a world renowned successful personality in your particular field of endeavour or someone whom you greatly admire and obtain their biography. Read through this biography over the course of the next month and then write down the qualities which he or she displayed in achieving their successes. You will then be in a position to compare those qualities with the strengths that you have already identified in Activity No. 22. (I believe you will be rather surprised to find how similar those lists turn out to be.)

What obstacles did he/she overcome in achieving his/her success(es)?

List the qualities which he/she displayed in achieving his/her success(es)

Self-motivation

Chapter 6

Key Learning Point

How to motivate yourself

Basic motivation involves a three phase cycle. There is always a need to start with, or desire if you prefer, that stimulates a behavioural response directed towards a goal which, once attained, then satisfies that need or desire.

Figure 4: Self-motivation

Let's take hunger as a simple everyday example to illustrate the point. When you are hungry you will have goal-directed behaviour. You will go to your refrigerator or stove, prepare your food and consume it. The consumption of the food, of course, is the goal which satisfies the hunger need. Everyone can relate to that – a straight forward biological need – and we do not have to do anything about resuscitating the need because our normal physiological system will ensure that we become hungry again automatically after a period of time. The point I want to emphasise is that a satisfied need is not a motivator of behaviour. This is important to realise when you are motivating yourself, because you have to initially establish and then continually re-establish the need or desire yourself if you are to become fully self motivated.

A satisfied need is not a motivator of behaviour

Key Learning Point

Cultivating desire

How do you cultivate that desire? Basically you focus on the rewards of the goal. You ask yourself three questions: 'What are the obstacles in my path to this goal?'; 'What are the rewards for me on attainment of the goal?' and 'Does the long-term pleasure to be derived outweigh the short-term pain in overcoming the obstacles?' This short-term 'pain' is the price to be paid in terms of time, effort and money. Does the expected return justify the investment? Once you have answered those questions you can decide whether your desire is strong enough. Bear in mind what was said in the very first chapter about the pain and pleasure principle. You will find that this principle, simplistic though it may seem, underlies your behaviour as your actions will be governed by your need to avoid pain or desire to gain pleasure. And remember your brain is programmed to do far more to avoid pain than to gain pleasure. So your desires and needs, in the form of your associations with pain or pleasure are the motivational forces within you. To change your behaviour (and, therefore, the results you produce in life), you must focus upon how not changing your existing behaviour will be more painful than changing it as well as how changing it will bring you pleasure in the long-term. Unfortunately most of us tend to do what we do for short-term pleasure or to avoid short-term pain rather than taking the correct view of visualising the long-term pain that will be avoided and the long-term pleasure that will be gained by changing our behaviour. To change our behaviour we have to change what we currently link to pleasure and pain. We do this by again utilising the autogenic conditioning technique.

Key Question

Key Learning Point

To change our behaviour we have to change what we currently link to pain and pleasure

Achievement motive versus fear of failure

Let's now look at the achievement motive versus the fear of failure. I am sure you will have experienced this at some stage in your life. You have probably been in positions where you wanted to achieve a certain goal, had developed a plan and taken action steps, but suddenly encountered obstacles which led you to start doubting your own abilities. You became anxious about the success of your project, and were no longer confident of its successful achievement. That is where the fear of failure entered the picture to remind you of past mistakes. This should have been the time for you to concentrate on what you wanted and not on what you did not want. You should have used the 'switching' technique. This involves controlling your own focus of thought and whenever you catch yourself thinking about the possibility of failure, you immediately direct your thoughts to ones of success. You have to bolster the achievement motive so that it completely outweighs the limiting fear of failure. You do this by focusing on your past successes and continually reminding yourself of the successful person you are. You can reflect right now on a period in your life when you felt really good about a certain achievement. Bring that back to mind and focus again on the feelings that you had at that time. See yourself as the winner that you were then and realise that you still have those same qualities now even though they may have been suppressed for a while. All you have to do is to re-use them – and realise that you have whatever you need to be a success. But, you must take action and give yourself the opportunity of exercising your qualities. Concentrate on your strengths, and delegate your weaknesses. Everybody has weaknesses. If you focus on them that is your choice but it will definitely hinder your progress. If you recognise that you have certain weaknesses that are preventing you from progressing at a much faster rate then, by all means, plan to transform them into strengths. People 'fail' because they neither recognise nor use the strengths which they possess and tend to dwell too much on their weaknesses and limitations.

Concentrate on your strengths and delegate your weaknesses

Key Learning Point

Six characteristics of self-motivated people

What are the characteristics of self-motivated people? There are six basic traits:

Action Checklist

1. Vision

Firstly, they have a *vision* of what they want. On a regular basis, they use their imagination which is a faculty largely ignored in our modern education system. Take, for example, an architect. How can a building be constructed without plans and without knowing the purpose of the building? The architect can't possibly draw the plans without knowing the purpose of the building and obviously the construction workers cannot start until they have a plan. So a *vision* of the end result is essential to stimulate the motivational drive to take the necessary action. The more clear-cut this VISION is, the stronger the motivational drive, and regular autogenic conditioning will develop this clarity of *vision*.

2. Self-confidence

The second characteristic of self-motivated people is that they have *self-confidence* and, as a result, a positive self-image. As this subject was fully covered in Chapter 5, no further elaboration is necessary here.

3. Positive mental attitude

A positive mental attitude is the third characteristic of self-motivated people. This attitude must be consistent with the person's self image. It is pointless having a positive attitude if at the same time he believes, perhaps subconsciously, that he is not worthy of his goals and therefore, holds on to an inadequate self-image. The two must be compatible. He must become solution orientated. All too often, when problems arise the tendency is to focus on the problem and start asking questions such as: 'Why did I get into this situation?', or 'Why does it always have to happen to me?' As mentioned in the previous chapter, if you continually ask yourself negative questions, your brain will search your memory bank and will come up with negative answers – it will tell you why you failed – in fact it will give you a choice of reasons. ('Because you are a 'dummy'; 'You are stupid', 'You failed at school','You have no money', and so on.) It will look for answers, the nature of which are pre-determined by the questions. Fortunately the converse also applies. When you ask positive questions, your brain will search for and come up with positive answers. You should develop the habit of starting every day by asking yourself certain questions which will help you focus on the positive aspects of your life and set the tone for the day ahead. Questions such as: 'What is great about my life right now?' 'What areas of my life are really satisfying?' 'Who can I compliment or praise today?' This power of asking the right questions is also the key to developing a success expectancy which is the fourth characteristic of self-motivated people.

Key Learning Point

The questions you regularly ask yourself determine your focus

4.   Success expectancy

Success expectancy comes about through having the right belief system. All self-motivated people have a belief that they can and will win. That initiates the expectancy of success which brings the law of attraction into play. When you believe you can do something and then expect it to happen – when you can visualise your goals as achieved on a regular basis – you start to attract to you the situations, people, ideas, suggestions and thoughts – that will move you towards your goals.

5.   Self-discipline

Self-discipline is the fifth vital characteristic of self motivated people. It is mental and physical toughness and needs regular exercise. Physical exercise helps build *self-discipline* on its own. But it is even more important to have regular mental exercise, in the form of daily autogenic conditioning – twice a day for 20 minutes each session. Relaxation also forms part of the process. Exercise and relaxation go hand in hand – they are both therapeutically beneficial as well as contributing towards developing your *self discipline*. They are two sides of the same coin.

6.   Persistence

The sixth and final characteristic and I believe the most important one of them all for self-motivated individuals is *persistence*. You must continue keeping on whenever it seems as though you are at a 'dead-end' or you have come up against obstacles that you can't immediately overcome. That is precisely the time when you have to keep going. So many people give up when they are within touching distance of their goal. It was Napoleon Hill who said: 'Winners never quit – quitters never win'. *Persistence* is vitally important. Where would we be today without people like Thomas Edison, (referred to in Chapter 5), who 'failed' 10,000 times, in his experiments to invent the electric light bulb? Now what would most people have done under the same circumstances? I am sure a lot would have given up after ten failures or a hundred, certainly after a thousand. But Edison didn't. His attitude was such that he was progressively eliminating the alternatives. He was looking for ways that worked and his 'failures' were seen as the ways that didn't work. With that attitude he could not possibly fail. Each so-called 'failure' was a learning experience in his mind; it was negative feedback from which he learned and then moved on, ensuring that whatever errors had been made were not repeated.

Persistence is a habit which becomes increasingly stronger the more you bring to mind the benefits that you will reap on successful achievement of your goals. In this context, persistence is another important by-product of regular autogenic conditioning. One of your goals should be to develop the habit of persistence. Any habit is cultivated by repetition. It follows that if you repeatedly use your imagination and willpower to ensure that you see each task, no matter how small, through to a successful conclusion you will be acquiring the habit of persistence which will become part of your automatic behavioural responses when pursuing your larger goals.

Strengthening your motivation

The strength of the motivational forces within you depends on the associations you have made, both consciously and unconsciously, with what causes you pain and pleasure. You can heighten your motivational drive by increasing the emotional intensity of these associations through autogenic conditioning. Bob Richards, one of America's motivational experts, was born with a club foot but overcame that disadvantage to the extent that he became an Olympic athlete. He subsequently became an outstanding public speaker and wanted to help others achieve their goals. He had a simple three phase formula for self-motivation: 'You are what you think; you are what you go for; and you are what you do'. Let's take those in sequence.

Key Learning Point

'You are what you think; you are what you go for; you are what you do'

Bob Richards

Firstly, 'You are what you think'. Virtually every chapter in this book mentions the power of thought, usually in the positive sense. But let me put a negative thought to you to illustrate a point. If I ask you not to think of an elephant, what immediately springs to mind? You can see that elephant in all its glory, can't you? There it is flapping its ears, in full colour. Now that is the power of thought. You see if you do not wish to focus on what you do not want, you will not succeed by telling yourself not to think about it. Instead you need to consciously switch your thoughts to what you do want — it is, after all, your choice. Your thoughts start the chain reaction effect. If you want a successful life it presupposes a continuing cycle of successful years, months, weeks and days, each successful day comprising a series of successful acts. So, by ensuring you do your best in whatever activity you happen to be performing at that moment, you are pre-ordaining a successful life, as there is a cause and effect relationship between thought and attitude, between attitude and behaviour, between behaviour and performance, between performance and results and finally between results and your life. Consequently, control over your thoughts will lead to control over your life. Self-motivation is based on the scientific principle that you become the product of your dominant thinking. You must, therefore, see how tremendously vital it is for you to control the thoughts that enter your mind.

Control over your thoughts will lead to control over your life

Key Learning Point

Secondly he said: 'You are what you go for'. That emphasises the significance of setting and striving for goals. It is impossible for you to become truly self-motivated without having written, challenging, specific, measurable and prioritised goals. They are essential for your ultimate success in life as who you become in the process of striving for your goals is far more important than the actual attainment of the goals themselves.

Bob Richards' third point was; 'You are what you do.' Here let me repeat again as I have done so often in this book – nothing is going to change in your life until you transfer principles and techniques into *action*. Whatever you have read in this book must be reinforced by the activities and exercises provided and be assimilated into your life by your daily actions. Use them every single day of your life. You must consciously and deliberately put these principles into practice for yourself because that is the only way that your desired results will come about. Nothing is ever going to happen without you **doing** something. By now you should have set your goals, developed a plan of action and transferred the prioritised action steps into your diary or 'To Do' list which you update daily. There is thus no reason (excuse?) not to go into action – so do it!

Key Management Concept

Neuro-Linguistic Programming (NLP)

Your results in life will be determined by your behaviour and your behaviour in turn is dictated by your state (a combination of your thoughts, feelings and attitude). If you were able to control this state and therefore ensure your most resourceful behaviour, then it follows that you would be able to consistently produce the results you desired. Well the good news is that you can. Neuro-Linguistic Programming (NLP) has given us some of the most powerful breakthrough techniques in personal development that I have encountered over the many years I have been associated with the subject. I honestly believe that NLP has done for personal development what the computer did for the business industry. However, I should add that there are now many strains of NLP and I certainly do not subscribe to a number of the off-shoots. Like anything else, you should take what you prove to yourself to be beneficial and discard that which does not work. This book is a compilation of different principles and techniques which I have proved over the years work and they come from a variety of different sources, NLP being one of them.

Key Learning Point

By controlling your state you can consistently produce the results you desire

Neuro-Linguistic Programming tells us that we represent any experience through a number of our senses but predominantly the three major senses of visual (sight), auditory (hearing) and kinesthetic (feelings). The other two senses, those of gustatory (taste) and olfactory (smell) are not considered part of the major representational system when dealing with state management.

Personal state management

The principle to be used in accessing your most motivated state is that of the stimulus/response. I'm sure you can remember back to your first love affair. Perhaps there is a piece of music which, when played, takes you back to those days and you can even remember for example the particular restaurant and the meal that you had and what your partner was wearing and even perhaps some of the conversation that took place on that evening. The music in this instance provides the stimulus or trigger. The experience is then represented in a visual, auditory and kinesthetic manner. So you would recall that experience by means of what you saw, what you heard and what you felt during the playing of that music at the restaurant.

The NLP theory is that if you can now formulate the composition of this motivational strategy from an experience that caused you to feel highly motivated, you can use this self same formula to motivate you to do what you would like to be motivated to do but which currently you are not.

The exercise involves casting your mind back to a time when you felt totally motivated. Ask yourself what was the very first thing that caused you to feel totally motivated? Perhaps it was something you saw, or something you heard, or something you felt? Whatever it was, write it down. Then ask yourself what was the very next thing that caused you to feel totally motivated? Was it something else that you saw, was it something else that you heard or was it something else that you felt? Write that down. Do this again for another couple of times or until such time as you feel you have fully recaptured that motivated state.

In between the questions you should ask yourself: 'On a scale of 0 – 100, 100 being totally motivated, where am I now?' Once you have answered in excess of 90 to that question, you should anchor that state with a physical stimulus. (NLP terminology uses 'trigger' and 'anchor' synonymously and both of them mean a stimulus. So initially, you are attempting to 'anchor' a state which you can later 'trigger' at will, by using some form of stimulus such as a clenched fist and punching the air and perhaps at the same time shouting out loudly 'YES'.)

Once you have established your trigger, you need to test it. You do this by breaking the pattern of your previous thoughts through focusing on something completely different. Then you activate the trigger and determine for yourself whether you have recaptured that totally motivated state. If you have, that is great. Then you need to repeat the exercise of breaking your thought pattern and reactivating your trigger at least six times today and then a further 12 times tomorrow until it has become automatic. If you found that activating the trigger did not recapture your totally motivated state then you need to go back again into the experience and play around with some of the representations. For example, if the first thing that caused you to feel totally motivated was something you saw, then bring that picture to mind and start manipulating that picture in your mind's eye. Generally speaking, if you make that picture bigger, more colourful, much clearer and you mentally transport yourself into the picture so that you become fully associated with it, your feelings should greatly intensify. (You need to prove this to yourself as some people – a minority – find that it works the opposite way with them.) In the same way you can manipulate an auditory representation by changing the sound – making it louder, giving it greater resonance and clarity. Similarly with a kinesthetic representation, you would enhance whatever feelings you had experienced at the time. You need to do this until you are able with absolute confidence to say that you are at least in excess of 90 per cent on your motivational scale.

There is a classic NLP term that is so appropriate to personal success: *'You lose what you don't use!'* It is one thing knowing how to access your most motivated state when you want to and having the necessary trigger to do so, but it is another thing entirely to apply it. So please practice using your trigger in actual situations where you need to be at your best and then determine the effectiveness of it. (Naturally, you do not have to physically punch the air and shout *'yes'* at the top of your voice just prior to a presentation to a board of directors! You can simply visualise yourself activating the trigger and your motivated state will be accessed.)

You lose what you don't use

Key Learning Point

Mirroring and matching

Another NLP technique which is highly beneficial in motivating yourself involves creating rapport with someone else. This is done by what is known as 'mirroring' or 'matching'. This basically involves mimicking the other person's body language in a subtle, non-threatening manner. When using the 'mirroring' technique, it is as if you are looking into a mirror and therefore you would replicate whatever the other person was doing with their left side of the body with your right side and vice versa. When 'matching' someone's body language, you would move the right side of your body into the positions adopted by the other person's right side. Initially, the body language should either be mirrored or matched (never a combination of the two) so that you are following, after a comfortable and appropriate time span, the body movements of the other person. This is known as 'pacing'. When you feel that you may have established rapport, you can check whether this has been achieved by 'leading' in body language movements and seeing whether the other person follows suit. As soon as they do, you know that you have achieved subconscious rapport and your client or customer is now very receptive to what you have to offer. The important point to remember in this exercise is the subtlety and timing of your movements so as not to make it blatantly obvious that you are copying every move the other person makes.

Values

Your values play an important role in your motivational level. You have positive, 'moving towards' values and simultaneously you hold negative – 'moving away from' or repelling values. It is essential for our eventual goal achievement that we do not have any conflict between the positive and negative values. For example, if your most important positive value was success and at the same time your most important negative value was the fear of failure or rejection, you have a major conflict and are most likely to sabotage your action steps *en route* to your goal. It is again the pain and pleasure principle coming into the picture. The answer in cases such as these is to understand that no true and meaningful success will come about without enduring a certain amount of short-term pain. This pain could be the sacrificing of time, effort or money, the possibility of embarrassment or humiliation, the risk of losing what you currently have and so on. You now need to link as much pain as you can to not taking the action steps which you have planned and then focus on the tremendous pleasure that will be gained from successful attainment of the goal.

Key Learning Point

You must eliminate any potential conflict between your positive and negative values to avoid sabotaging your action steps

Decision making

To motivate yourself continuously, you need to become an effective decision maker. The way to do this is to make more decisions. The more decisions you make the better you will become at making them. You may well make a number of bad decisions initially but these should be seen as the learning experiences that they are. Of course, you should do what you can to avoid repeating those same mistakes. However, you will never become a good decision maker by vacillating over decisions or by waiting until you have the full set of facts in front of you.

To become an effective decision maker – make more decisions

Key Learning Point

An effective decision making method and a very simple one is the PMI technique. This is where you would take a sheet of paper and divide it into three columns and head the first column with 'P' which represents the positive points of the matter you are going to decide upon, 'M' the minus points associated with the matter and 'I' the interesting points. Once you have listed all the positives, minuses and interesting points, you need to place a value to each one of them. In other words give each point a rating on a one to five basis. So, for example, you would rank your positive points on the basis of their value to you on a scale of one to five. They would be contrasted with the minus points which would have a negative rating, also on a one to five scale depending on how detrimental they would be to the outcome of the matter. Where the positives and the minuses almost balance each other, then the interesting points could be taken into consideration and here you can give each interesting point either a positive or a negative rating and then add those up. This is obviously a very logical way of making decisions. My advice to you is that you bring in right brain and once the logical decision has been made, do some autogenic conditioning and attempt to visualise and emotionalise the decision in force. This will help you to get some intuitive feeling about the decision.

Activity

Key Learning Point

Always make your decisions on your vision of what you want rather than on fears of what you do not want

Reframing

Another effective NLP technique that you can use to motivate yourself is reframing. Reframing means changing the point of view that you take to a particular situation. You will know that if you change your representation or perception of a situation and its subsequent meaning, that will alter, in an instant, your state and therefore your behaviour. You can reframe situations by changing the context or the content. Context reframing involves taking a negative situation and showing how the same behaviour or experience could be highly beneficial in another context. Content reframing involves taking the same situation and changing its meaning. It was Dr. Albert Ellis, the founder of Rational Emotive Therapy who brought to prominence the important point that it is not the activating event which causes us to react in a certain way but it is more the perception of the meaning of that event, in other words our beliefs about what that event means to us that stimulates our reaction. This means that we can greatly alter whatever negative behaviours we may have to certain situations by seeing the meaning of them differently. Reframing the initial stimulus changes the message that you are sending to your brain and consequently the responses that flow from it.

Summary

1. Basic motivation involves a three phase cycle – a need or desire, goal directed behaviour and the goal itself.

2. A satisfied need is not a motivator of behaviour.

3. The cultivation and fuelling of desire is brought about by the regular use of autogenic conditioning utilising the pain/pleasure principle.

4. You can control thoughts of failure by focusing on past successes and expected future ones.

5. There are six character traits of self-motivated people. They have:

    a) A vision of what they want.

    b) Self-confidence.

    c) A positive mental attitude.

    d) A success expectancy.

    e) Self-discipline.

    f) Persistence.

6. Neuro-Linguistic Programming offers simple yet powerful techniques for personal state management. By linking a highly motivated state with a stimulus, future activation of that stimulus automatically accesses that state.

7. You can improve your communication skills through body language rapport using NLP techniques like 'matching' and 'mirroring'.

8. Your motivational level will be affected by the values that you hold, both positive and negative. The positive values will tend to attract you whilst the negative values will repel you. Your behaviour is then determined by the amount of pain or pleasure you link to these values.

9. To become a better decision maker make decisions more often. Any bad decisions will provide the learning experiences that will equip you to make better decisions in the future. Try to make decisions quickly and change them rarely. Use of the 'PMI' technique can greatly assist decision making.

10. You can enhance your motivational level by using another NLP technique known as 'reframing'. This means changing the point of view that you take to a particular situation through altering either the content or the context.

If this is your first reading of this book, please proceed to Chapter 7. If this is your second or subsequent reading, please carry out Activities 27, 28, 29, 30 and 31.

Activity

Determining the true reasons for desiring your goals

You know by now that, when contemplating personal goals, the '*why*?' is far more important than the '*how*?' To sustain your motivational drive at a high level you need to be continuously aware of the reasons for desiring your goals.

Therefore, on the sheets provided, write down all the reasons you can think of for wanting to achieve your goals. Do this for your four major goals. Try to come up with at least five reasons for each goal.

Once you are satisfied that you have all the compelling reasons for desiring your goals that you can think of, go back to your plans of action for each of your four major goals (Activity No. 9) and ensure that your 'Rewards and Benefits on Successful Attainment' section is revised, where necessary, to take account of all your reasons.

Statement of goal No. ____

_____

_____

_____

Reasons for desiring this goal (as detailed as possible)

1 _____

_____

_____

2 _____

_____

_____

3 _____

_____

_____

4 _____

_____

_____

5 _____

_____

_____

Use this format for goal Nos. 1-4.

Developing persistence

Persistence is a habit which, like any other habit, is cultivated through the repetition of a number of conscious acts. To develop persistence, the following acts must be repeated over the course of the next month:

1. Refining of your major written goals. You will be performing autogenic conditioning (creative visualisation sessions) twice daily and will therefore be crystallising the pictures of your major goals. **You should rewrite all your major goals daily for 30 consecutive days.** (See Activity No. 10).

2. Revise your written plans of action. Flexibility is the key here. As you refine your goals daily so you should change your written plans to attain them. (See Activity No. 9).

3. During your daily autogenic conditioning periods, you should focus on the rewards and benefits of successful attainment of your goals. This sustains your motivational drive at a high level, and develops persistence.

4. Daily associations with people who will encourage and support your goal directed efforts.

5. Record and review all your successes daily. (Use your two-page-per-day diary or your 'To Do' list). (See Activity No. 18.)

Activity

Activity No. 29

Compiling your own job description

Use the format outlined to write (or re-write) your job description as you would like to see it, taking into account your company's (or your particular department's) major objectives and your own mix of academic qualifications, acquired skills and experience. Then show it to your manager for his/her comment/approval/authorisation.

(Ensure you include signature blocks for both yourself and your manager on your job description.)

see over

Job description for

_____

Position in company

_____

Major goal No. 1 (one of the reasons for the job's creation)

_____

_____

_____

Performance specifications (This breaks the major goal down into specific, measurable sub-goals with deadlines and, wherever possible, quantifiable performance standards)

_____

_____

_____

_____

_____

_____

_____

(Self)   (Manager)

(Produce your own additional sheets for each major work goal)

Activity No. 30

Accessing your most resourceful state

You will know that your results are determined by your behaviour which depends, to a large extent, on the state of mind that you are in at that particular moment. This activity is designed to show you how you can initially 'anchor' a resourceful state you have had in the past and then 'trigger' or activate this state whenever you choose in the future.

Seat yourself in the position you would normally assume for your autogenic conditioning sessions. Close your eyes and focus upon a significant achievement in your past. It doesn't matter how far back you need to go but it must be an achievement which made you feel really satisfied and proud of yourself. (Refer to Activity No.22.)

Now experience the sensations of that achievement again. Try to use as many of your senses as you can to re-live the feelings that you had at that time. When you feel you have recaptured the peak of that feeling, 'anchor' that state by clenching your fist, punching the air and simultaneously shouting 'YES!'. (Naturally, it is advisable to carry out this exercise in private and where you cannot be overheard! Additionally, you may wish to choose your own 'trigger' which may be different to the clenched fist punching the air. Whatever 'trigger' you choose, ensure that it is unique – in other words, it is not a physical gesture that you make often.)

Now think of something completely different – the latest news headlines, the weather, the results of your favourite sports team, what you plan to do today or tomorrow etc.

Now activate your 'trigger' and see what happens. You should immediately change your state back to that satisfied and proud feeling. If this does not happen, then you need to go back to the initial establishment of that feeling.

To reinforce this state management ability, activate your 'trigger' at least 6 times today and repeat the exercise another 12 times tomorrow, each time recapturing the peak feeling that you had in the past. It is important to break your pattern between each one of these activations by simply thinking of something else as suggested above.

There is an old Buddhist saying: 'To know and not to use is not yet to know.' You will find this state management technique to be of tremendous value to you, **provided you use it regularly**. If you do not make regular use of it, it will lose its effectiveness. In the same way that your physical muscles will atrophy if they are not regularly used, so will your abilities to control your state. So look for instances daily where you would like to perform at your best and then use the 'triggering' mechanism to activate that state.

Incidentally, you do not have to physically manifest your 'trigger' for it to be effective. Provided you can visualise yourself carrying it out, the effects will be the same.

Activity No. 31

Activity

Pain and pleasure associations

1. Write down your most important major goal.

_____

_____

2. How will you feel on successful attainment of this goal?

_____

_____

3. Write down the four most important activities that have to be performed for you to attain this goal.

    a)   Activity No. 1 :

_____

_____

    b)   Activity No. 2 :

_____

_____

    c)   Activity No. 3 :

_____

_____

    d)   Activity No. 4 :

_____

_____

4. Now describe the 'pain' (the possible cost to you in time, effort or money, the risk involved, the chances of being rejected, embarrassed or humiliated, etc) which you have previously associated with performing these activities.

    _____

    _____

    _____

    _____

5. Now describe the 'pleasure' (remaining in your comfort zone, avoiding risk, having time, effort and money for alternative pursuits, etc) which you have previously associated with NOT performing these activities.

    _____

    _____

    _____

6. Now visualise yourself in the future having not performed any of these activities and consequently not having attained your goal. How will you feel then? Associate as much pain as you can to this possibility. Fully describe the extent of the pain you (and your loved ones) will experience if you do NOT perform these activities.

    _____

    _____

    _____

7. Now refer back to 2. above and remind yourself of the tremendous pleasure for you (and your loved ones) that will result following your successful completion of the activities. Carry out autogenic conditioning and visualise the successful attainment of the goal. Intensify your feelings by making the picture on the screen of your mind bigger, clearer, more colourful and by fully associating yourself with it. Do this by mentally transporting yourself into the picture and experiencing with all of your senses the pleasurable feelings of achievement, excitement, euphoria, pride, happiness, etc. Write down these feelings. Add to your feelings in 2.

    _____

    _____

    _____

8. Use these associations regularly, initially to remind yourself of WHY you are doing what you are doing and then, most importantly, to develop the habit of a consistently high level of self-motivation (drive).

How to motivate others

In any organisation, its people are its most important assets and to obtain significant improvements in productivity entails getting the best out of those people. Unfortunately, if we look around at the number of industrial disturbances and the instances of constant bickering between management and employees, it is obvious that a large part of the productivity problem can be attributed to management and supervisors not fully understanding how to handle their people. They seem to have a habit of constantly rubbing their employees up the wrong way, often for apparently no good reason.

In my experience with training companies over the years, I am amazed that so little attention is paid to the skill of handling subordinates. Even in business schools, where you would expect a lot of emphasis to be placed on this subject, it is largely ignored.

The abilities to interact with people and clearly communicate your ideas are essential prerequisites to motivating others. If you have ambitions to run a large organisation sometime in the future, you will definitely need these two skills as part of your managerial make-up.

Personal example

Key Management Concept

A key factor in dealing successfully with others is the example you portray on a regular basis.

*It is not so much what you **know** but what you **do** that counts in the eyes of your subordinates*

Setting a good personal example goes a long way to creating the right climate for employees to become self-motivated. It is not enough to tell your employees what to do. You need to be able to show them and that what you are asking them to do is certainly no more than you are prepared to do yourself.

The authority you have by virtue of your managerial position may well force your subordinates to work for you. However, if, in addition to this authority, you are able to display leadership characteristics by setting the right example, by being able to persuade them and guide them rather than coerce them, you will get far more out of them and willingly so. Most people will actually perform better when asked for their co-operation rather than by direct orders to perform a certain way.

Attention

If you are a manager with a realistic span of control, having say between seven and ten subordinates beneath you, you should be in a position to pay personal attention to each one of them. Even though some of them may not be doing as interesting a job as others or be making the same contributions to the company's goals, they still require attention if they are to perform at their best. You know yourself how important it is to receive praise and appreciation for a job well done – or encouragement and support for a job about to be done. That is what personal attention is all about and everybody needs it. In the same way that machinery needs regular servicing and lubrication, so your employees require personal attention in the form of appreciation and praise on a regular basis.

Key Management Concept

Employees require personal attention in the form of appreciation and praise on a regular basis for them to be constantly motivated

People will want to work for you and give of their best if you pay attention to them as individuals and appreciate their importance to you and the company as a whole. When you are supporting them and helping them to grow within the organisation, constantly looking for ways of improving their abilities and increasing their responsibilities, you will have a highly motivated team.

Praisings and reprimands

A fundamental rule to observe when trying to maximise the output of your staff is to 'praise publicly and criticise privately'. We all need and enjoy pats on the back regularly and unfortunately it is a common tendency to overlook the excellent work that people do whilst at the same time, be quick to criticise any substandard work performed. The emphasis should always be on praising your subordinates rather than reprimanding them. However, it is part of a leaders make-up to also know exactly when and how to reprimand subordinates.

Key Management Concept

Praise publicly and criticise privately

For you to be an effective manager and get the best from your staff you need to establish a feedback system whereby their performance can be accurately measured. This follows the basic behavioural modification process where successful performances are encouraged and reinforced, and errors and mistakes pointed out as they arise. It's important, from a motivational point of view, to know that it is wrong to reprimand people who do not meet their goals until they have proven competent at attaining them. Up to that point it is a training problem. However, once they have demonstrated competence in attaining the goals commensurate with the performance specifications, and subsequently slip up, that is when the reprimand should be given. The reprimand should criticise the deed and not the doer. In the same way that you motivate your child by pointing out that his or her behaviour at some stage was not acceptable, and therefore would not criticise the child himself or herself as this would have negative consequences, so you would focus on the subordinate's behaviour at that time, without degrading him/her as a person. Any reprimand should always finish with a re-affirmation of your confidence in his/her ability to perform the task, as previously demonstrated.

Any reprimand should criticise the deed not the doer

Key Management Concept

As part of a motivational programme, regular performance appraisals should be held. (The periodicity would depend on the size of the company but usually performance appraisals should be held twice a year.) On these occasions there should be no surprises as, provided the individual has a signed copy of the job description, he/she should know exactly how they have been performing and the performance appraisal period should be an opportunity to reinforce encouragement already given and to discuss and reset goals which need to be added to or amended on the job description.

Goals and job descriptions

Key Management Concept

Strictly speaking when we talk about motivating others it's actually a misnomer. We can't really motivate other people. What we can do is create a climate within which people will become self-motivated. But how do we create this climate? It's quite simple really. If we look at what motivates ourselves we understand that we can't be truly motivated unless we have desirable goals and are continuously aware of our reasons for pursuing them. It's the same for those working for us or our company. If they are to become fully motivated we must realise that they also have goals in their lives and they will work for us far more readily if we can show them how they can obtain those goals through the achievement of our company objectives. So we must understand the wants and needs of other people before we can ever hope to create this climate of motivation.

Goals in the workplace pre-suppose that a job description exists which outlines the responsibilities and performance specifications of the different jobs. Ideally, the individuals themselves should be involved in the compilation of these job descriptions. However, this is not always possible as often, the job descriptions have been tailored to a particular individual's strengths and then, when he or she leaves the company, the same job description is used for the next incumbent. In these cases, the new employee should be given the existing job description as a guideline and, after three months, be invited to participate in the review of that job description. This participation greatly increases the commitment to the goals outlined in that job description.

It is far easier to retain a high level of morale in your company when your subordinates are busy most of the time. Where they have time on their hands and tend to get bored, dissatisfaction sets in and morale drops. Consequently, the job description plays a key role in motivating others and ensuring that morale remains high. The job description should be wide enough in scope to ensure that the individual is constantly busy.

Positive attitude

When dealing with your subordinates, it pays handsome dividends to be in a positive frame of mind. By greeting your subordinates with a pleasant smile and adopting a respectful attitude, you will gain respect and loyalty in return. Try treating your subordinates the same way that you would treat your customers and just see the difference in their responses and in their performance levels.

Key Management Concept

Treat your subordinates the way you want them to treat your customers

Generally, people will work for someone who shows them a friendly manner but which is backed by firmness and authority when necessary. A good leader should never be manipulated by his or her subordinates as this is a blatant sign of weakness. However, you do not have to be a tough, arrogant, ruthless unapproachable manager to obtain best results. You should develop the ability to be friendly with your subordinates without losing your authority.

A sense of humour is a good characteristic for any leader to have. However, it can be a two edged sword. If you can laugh and have fun with your subordinates rather than at them, you will certainly endear yourself to them.

Future role of managers

Management in the past has been a combination of both getting work done through others – your team of subordinates – and doing certain tasks yourself. I believe this will shortly change and that managers of the future will concentrate solely on getting work done through others. Their main function will then be to encourage and support their team to achieve objectives rather than performing tasks personally without the team. This pre-supposes that managers of the future will have to have a comprehensive understanding of human behaviour and receive training in the effective ways of maximising results from a team.

Appreciation

Everybody likes to feel important and you should remind your employees occasionally of how important they are to the company. I believe one of the best ways of showing your appreciation to an individual is to follow up the verbal praise with a simple hand written note. This indicates the sincerity of your feelings as you have taken the time and trouble to compile the note.

Key Management Concept

Guide to Best Practice

Follow up verbal praise with a simple handwritten note

Communication

Motivation in the workplace is also greatly enhanced by two-way communication channels. You need to elicit your staff's opinions about any work problems they may have and encourage open communication between themselves and management. When subordinates know that they have direct access to you and that the information which is fed back to you is acted upon, they will be more inclined to initiate ideas on improving productivity or saving costs and letting you know about them.

When communicating with subordinates, it is often a good idea to follow up verbal instructions with written memos as reminders. However, try to avoid communicating solely by memos as this becomes extremely impersonal and carries far less weight than a one-on-one verbal communication.

Many managers take the view that communicating with their subordinates is uni-directional, with them (the managers) doing most of the talking. If you are not prepared to listen intently and seriously to their problems then you may well find in time that you will have nothing to listen to because they will have lost all interest in discussing items of concern with you. When they adopt this attitude and believe that you do not care, you have a major morale problem looming. When listening seriously to the problems of your subordinates, try always to appreciate their point of view – their hopes and aspirations as well as their concerns. By putting yourself in their shoes you are better placed to resolve the issues. Remember that the whole idea is to work towards a 'win-win' situation and this generally requires a 'give-give' relationship between you and your subordinates.

Many errors that are made by subordinates come as a result of not understanding correctly the instructions that were given to them. You as a leader should ensure that what you are attempting to communicate to them has been fully understood. Therefore when issuing instructions or orders which you need carried out and which are important for the success of the particular project, ensure that you obtain the feedback before any action is commenced. Also as mentioned previously it does help to have these instructions and orders in written format to back-up your verbal orders. When obtaining this feedback, ask relevant questions of your subordinates to ensure that they fully understand what is required. When important information is conveyed to subordinates, it is essential that this is repeated several times and perhaps in different forms i.e. verbally, by asking questions, by sending confirming memos, by setting deadlines for sub-goal achievements and the like. People do not remember everything you tell them in a single hearing. They need to hear it several times and then to digest that information.

A feedback mechanism is essential for effective communication

Key Management Concept

Meetings

Regular meetings with your employees, or a representative of those employees, where minutes of the meeting are taken and subsequently distributed to each employee showing the points raised and the action to be taken on them with specific deadlines included, goes a long way to improving the morale of your workforce. They need to be kept well informed about the happenings within the company and you need to be listening carefully to any suggestions they make for improvements. They need to be encouraged to make these suggestions. In many companies, management seem to feel that **they** are best equipped to solve the company problems. This is not necessarily the case and often the better

Guide to Best Practice

ideas will come from the workforce. Regular meetings will encourage the flow of such ideas.

To gain commitment from members of your staff, you should, wherever possible, invite their participation particularly in decisions that will affect them. If you hold regular meetings to discuss the direction in which the department is moving and any changes that are envisaged by management and elicit their opinion and feedback on these proposals, you will find that many good ideas are generated because they now feel part of the decision making process.

Key Management Concept

Participation in the decision making process will result in a high level of commitment

Responsibility and authority

It is essential when allocating responsibilities to individuals as part of their job description, that the necessary authority is also delegated to them. It is completely demotivational to expect your subordinates to be responsible for certain activities without giving them the necessary authority to carry them out.

Support, trust and confidence

When you are in charge of a team you must give them support. Although you may well have delegated responsibilities to different individuals, you always remain ultimately responsible for your department's results. This means that you must accept the blame if any of your subordinates do not satisfactorily perform their tasks. In the same way that you would expect to share the credit when your subordinates achieve departmental targets, so you should be prepared to 'carry the can' when they fall short of them.

If one of your subordinates obviously has some problem which is adversely affecting their ability to perform at their normal level, you as the leader need to tackle this immediately. If you can display genuine willingness to help them overcome that problem, you will earn their respect. If you do not act immediately, there is a good chance that the problem could 'mushroom' out of all proportion. To become a competent leader therefore you need to develop the ability to detect problems early and resolve them quickly.

You will find that your subordinates are much more highly motivated when you show trust and confidence in their abilities. When they realise that you are on their side and are there to support them in their endeavours, they will go out of their way to earn the trust that you have bestowed upon them. It follows that you also need to prove to them that they can trust you. If they know by your actions that you are continuously supporting them and giving them a fair say in the operation of the department, you will win their trust. You may, of course, find the exceptions who do not respond to your showing of confidence and trust in them. If they are not producing the results, give serious thought to dispensing with their services. You do not need them on your team.

Your subordinates will be much more highly motivated when you show trust and confidence in their abilities

Key Management Concept

Developing subordinates

As a manager or leader you are responsible for developing one or more of your subordinates to take over in the event that you are incapacitated for any reason. Equally, you should encourage your subordinates to develop people beneath them who could accede to their position should they be promoted. In this manner your department will grow far quicker than by protecting your position.

Incentive and fear motivation

You have heard of incentive and fear-type motivation – the 'carrot and stick' philosophy. Both of these work to a limited extent depending on prevailing circumstances. In economically tough times both incentive and fear motivation will produce better results than when money is not a major constraint. But, generally speaking, the 'carrot and stick' approach works only for as long as the donkey has an appetite for carrots or until he becomes numb from being beaten by the stick! It is the same with humans. Incentives and fear of being penalised or losing your job do not work in the long-term.

Key Management Concept

Incentive and fear motivation are not effective in the long-term. Incentives need to be part of a wider motivational philosophy regarded as 'fair' by employees

Administrative paperwork

A lot of managers find that their ability to manage subordinates is inhibited by the amount of paperwork that they are required to perform. If you find this to be the case, make sure you start delegating some of that administrative work. It should never interfere with your main task of personal supervision and support. Excess paperwork can become the bane of your life as it seems to unobtrusively eat in to increasingly more of your time – if you let it.

Every 90 days you should review your activities and delegate any that do not fall under the category of 'key activities'.

Situational leadership

When managing others, the leadership style that you adopt with them should be determined by the developmental level that they have reached in that particular situation. Basically, there are four leadership styles, namely: *directing, coaching, supporting* and *delegating*.

Directing

The directing style is very autocratic involving a lot of direction and close supervision from the leader with no decision making responsibilities being delegated to any subordinates. Instructions are given both on what is to be done as well as on how it is to be accomplished.

Coaching

The coaching style combines direction with supporting behaviour and input from the subordinate is sought in the form of ideas or suggestions but decision making is retained by yourself, the leader. Where sound ideas are raised, these are supported by the leader to reinforce the initiative of the subordinates.

Supporting

The supporting style differs from the coaching style in that there is now far less direction from the leader who facilitates and supports the attainment of goals by the subordinates. Decision making then is a shared responsibility between the leader and his/her subordinates.

Delegating

The final style, delegating, is where the authority and responsibility for decision making are delegated to the subordinates and very little direction or support from the leader is deemed necessary.

The different styles presuppose that the leader has the skills and abilities to know when a particular style is needed, to have the flexibility to use that particular style and to obtain the understanding of his/her subordinates of the reasons for using that particular style.

Developmental levels

The directing style of leadership is used when the subordinate lacks the relevant skills and experience but is highly motivated.

The coaching style is used where the subordinate lacks motivation as well as the necessary skills and experience. Direction is still required to improve the level of competence and support in the form of praise, encouragement and creating a climate in which the subordinate will feel free to offer ideas and suggestions.

The supporting style is used where the subordinate has the necessary skills and experience but where the motivation and confidence levels are lacking. In this situation, the subordinate requires a lot of support in bolstering confidence and re-stimulating motivation.

In the delegating style, the subordinate now has the knowledge, skills, experience, self-confidence and motivation to accept responsibility for all the decision making related to that situation.

Whilst the above advice on situational leadership and the use of varying styles might seem idealistic and impracticable, it is most definitely a worthwhile pursuit of anyone desirous of leading others effectively. Many leaders have the personal charisma and innate ability to lead others comfortably. However, the majority of aspiring leaders need to develop their talents along the way and situational leadership is an excellent framework for this development.

Summary

Key Learning Points

1. In any organisation, its people are the most important assets. The abilities to deal with people and clearly communicate your ideas are essential prerequisites to motivating others.

2. It is not so much what you KNOW but rather what you DO that counts in the eyes of your subordinates.

3. Most people will actually perform better when asked for their co-operation rather than by direct orders to perform a certain way.

4. Your employees require personal attention in the form of appreciation and praise on a regular basis.

5. Praise publicly and criticise privately.

6. Never reprimand subordinates who do not meet their goals until they have proven competent at attaining them.

7. When reprimanding a subordinate, always criticise the deed and not the doer. The reprimand should finish with a re-affirmation of your confidence in his/her ability.

8. Carry out regular performance appraisals using the job description as the basis. (At least two per year.)

9. To create a climate within which your subordinates will become self-motivated, find out their wants and needs – then help them to satisfy them.

10. Involve your subordinates in the compilation or review of their job descriptions.

11. Treat your subordinates in the same way that you would treat your customers and notice the difference in their performance levels.

12. Managers jobs in the future will have a much greater emphasis on getting results from others and will require a comprehensive understanding of human behaviour.

13. Develop the ability to be friendly with your subordinates without losing your authority. Laugh with them not at them.

14. Show appreciation by following up your verbal praise with a simple handwritten note.

15. Ensure that your subordinates have direct access to you and that you feed back to them the answers to any enquiries conveyed to you.

16. Follow up verbal instructions with written memos, but avoid communicating solely by memos.

17. You can develop a 'Win-Win' situation by cultivating a 'Give-Give' relationship between you and your subordinates.

18. Ensure your subordinates know exactly what is required by you. People do not remember everything you tell them in a single hearing. They need to hear it several times and then to digest that information.

19. Hold regular meetings with your staff and invite their participation on matters that affect them. Make sure you give them feed back on any proposals they submit.

20. When delegating responsibilities to subordinates, ensure that the commensurate authority is also delegated.

21. Show trust and confidence in your subordinates ability. They will trust you when your actions are consistent with your promises.

22. Develop a plan for growing your subordinates – a succession plan for every key position.

23. Incentive and fear motivation do not work in the long-term. Long lasting motivation comes from within the subordinates themselves – when they want to work for their department's goals.

24. Administrative paperwork should never inhibit your ability to manage subordinates. If it does, delegate it.

25. Situational leadership outlines four leadership styles: directing, coaching, supporting and delegating. It presupposes that the manager has the skills and abilities to know when a particular style is needed and to have the flexibility to use that style and ensure his or her subordinates understand the reasons for using that style in any particular situation. The different styles are used in different situations – at the various developmental levels of the subordinates.

If this is your first reading of this book, please proceed to Chapter 8. If this is your second or subsequent reading, please carry out Activities 32, 33 and 34.

Activity No. 32

Establishing your subordinates' reasons for working for you

You know that in order to create a climate within which your subordinates will become self-motivated it is necessary to discover their reasons for working for you. What do they want to be, do, or have in their lives? How can you then assist them to realise those desires?

Interview your subordinates individually and explain the purpose of the meeting. Then attempt to identify their four major goals. Ask similar questions and go through the same procedures as you did for setting your own goals. (Refer to Activities 7, 8 and 9). Use the sheets provided and, at the end of the interview, ensure that your subordinate has a copy, as well as you, which will assist in your follow-up.

Subordinates name:	Date:
Major goals	Deadline for achievement
1. _____	_____
2. _____	_____
3. _____	_____
4. _____	_____

Reasons for desiring the goals (as detailed as possible)

Goal No. 1:

_____

_____

_____

Goal No. 2:

_____

_____

_____

Goal No. 3:

_____

_____

_____

Goal No. 4:

_____

_____

_____

Activity No. 33

Leadership characteristics questionnaire

The 48 questions on the following questionnaire relate to 16 qualities generally associated with leaders. It is not, of course, an exhaustive list but will certainly give you a good indication of your strengths as well as the qualities to work on for you to become an effective leader. By ticking the appropriate space, answer the questions as quickly as you can, bearing in mind that the first answer that you think of is usually the most accurate. Then award yourself marks as allocated on the evaluation sheet provided.

Analysis of leadership characteristics

	Yes	No	Sometimes

A) COURAGE

1. Are you always prepared to take positive action to give effect to decisions?

2. Are you often frightened of the consequences of your actions?

3. Do you always face obstacles bravely and take action to overcome them?

B) SELF-CONFIDENCE

4. Are you generally optimistic concerning your own capacity for accomplishment?

Yes	No	Sometimes

5. Do you become flustered when confronted with a trying situation?

6. Do you tend towards timidity or have feelings of self doubt in your work situation?

C) SELF-CONTROL

7. Are you able to control your emotions and see things logically in stressful situations?

8. Do you discipline yourself to follow your plan to attain your goals?

9. Do you always finish what you set out to do?

D) SENSE OF RESPONSIBILITY

10. Are you sufficiently mature and capable to discharge difficult or exacting duties?

11. Can you perform tasks effectively despite unforeseen obstacles?

12. Do you readily take the blame or the credit for the results of a job over which you had control?

E) PERSUASIVE SKILLS

13. Can you get others to do things by appealing to reason?

14. Are you generally successful in urging people to act as you wish them to act?

	Yes	No	Sometimes

15. Are you easily deviated from your course of action by others?

F) SENSE OF JUSTICE

16. Do you insist on fair play?

17. Do you judge the actions of others by an objective set of ethical standards?

18. Do you believe it is often expedient to disregard moral and legal standards?

G) DECISIVENESS

19. Do you find it difficult to say 'No'?

20. Do you make decisions quickly and change your mind rarely?

21. Do you take time to make decisions and then at times change them rapidly?

H) SYMPATHY

22. Are you consistently just and considerate in your dealings with others?

23. Do you take little or no interest in the affairs of others within your group?

24. Do others come to you for advice on their personal problems?

	Yes	No	Sometimes

I) CO-OPERATION

25. Are you a good team man/woman who works well in harmony with others?

26. Are you difficult to work with or tend to be obstructive?

27. Do you encourage participation?

J) PERSONALITY

28. Are you a cheerful, enthusiastic, and optimistic person?

29. Do you have an adequate self-image?

30. Are you regarded as being a person of good character?

K) ENTHUSIASM

31. Are you eager and willing to become involved in activities around you?

32. Do you generally express favourable responses to your experiences?

33. Are you often apathetic or impassive towards new ideas?

L) DEFINITENESS OF PLANS TO ATTAIN GOALS

34. Do you have a written plan of action to attain your goals?

35. Do you change your plans often?

36. Do you operate on guesswork?

	Yes	No	Sometimes

M) MASTERY OF DETAIL

37. Do you investigate matters thoroughly before making decisions?

38. Do you tend to see things from different points of view?

39. Are you prone to inattentiveness?

N) PERSISTENCE

40. Do you see all jobs through without letting obstacles deter you?

41. Do you welcome problems and see them as challenges?

42. Do you interpret temporary setbacks as insurmountable obstacles?

O) INITIATIVE

43. Are you able to solve problems by finding whatever means are available and adapting them accordingly?

44. Do others regard you as resourceful and come to you for ideas?

45. Do you seek advice from others before attempting to find solutions yourself?

P) IMAGINATION

46. Are you a creative thinking person often coming up with original ideas?

	Yes	No	Sometimes
47. Are you able to vividly visualise the results of your actions?			
48. Do you think analytically or convergently, always seeking one answer to the problem?			

Evaluation of leadership questionnaire

CHARACTERISTIC	QUESTION No.	YES	NO	SOMETIMES
A) COURAGE	1	4	0	0
	2	0	4	2
	3	4	0	2
B) SELF-CONFIDENCE	4	4	0	2
	5	0	4	1
	6	0	4	1
C) SELF-CONTROL	7	4	0	2
	8	4	0	2
	9	4	0	2
D) SENSE OF RESPONSIBILITY	10	4	0	2
	11	4	0	2
	12	4	0	2
E) PERSUASIVE SKILLS	13	4	0	2
	14	4	0	2
	15	0	4	0
F) SENSE OF JUSTICE	16	4	0	0
	17	4	0	2
	18	0	4	0
G) DECISIVENESS	19	0	4	2
	20	4	0	2
	21	0	4	2

CHARACTERISTIC	QUESTION No.	YES	NO	SOMETIMES
H) SYMPATHY	22	4	0	1
	23	0	4	1
	24	4	0	2
I) CO-OPERATION	25	4	0	2
	26	0	4	0
	27	4	0	2
J) PERSONALITY	28	4	0	2
	29	4	0	2
	30	4	0	2
K) ENTHUSIASM	31	4	0	2
	32	4	0	2
	33	0	4	1
L) DEFINITENESS OF PLANS TO ATTAIN GOALS	34	4	0	2
	35	2	4	2
	36	0	4	2
M) MASTERY OF DETAIL	37	4	0	2
	38	4	0	2
	39	0	4	1
N) PERSISTENCE	40	4	0	1
	41	4	0	2
	42	0	4	0

CHARACTERISTIC	QUESTION No.	YES	NO	SOMETIMES
O) INITIATIVE	43	4	0	2
	44	4	0	2
	45	0	4	2
P) IMAGINATION	46	4	0	2
	47	4	0	2
	48	0	4	2

Evaluation per characteristic

8 or more: adequate for success.

Less than 8: requires improvement. If you are a leader or aspire to a leadership position and have scored less than 8 on any of the 16 characteristics, then building these qualities should become one of your personal development goals.

Activity No. 34

Activity

Developing your own leadership characteristics

Having completed Activity No. 33 and evaluated your results, you may have identified certain leadership characteristics which need strengthening.

You now need to build these into your goal setting exercise and your daily autogenic conditioning sessions as well as recording your own suggestions for accelerating the development of these characteristics.

Leadership characteristics to be strengthened	Action taken

How to develop and sustain a positive mental attitude

Chapter 8

An American survey carried out some years ago to determine the success qualities amongst Fortune 500 top entrepreneurs, discovered that there were four outstanding characteristics: IQ (intelligence quotient), academic knowledge, acquired skills and attitude. You would probably agree that there is nothing surprising in those results. In fact, you may well have come up with a similar combination had you been part of the exercise. However, what was surprising was the fact that 93 per cent of the entrepreneurs interviewed, attributed their success to attitude over and above any of the other three qualities.

William James, perhaps the best known of America's psychologists said: 'The greatest discovery of my generation is that man can change his life by changing his attitude of mind.' In a similar vein, Dr. Karl Menninger said: 'Attitudes are more important than facts.'

Key Learning Point

Man can change his life by changing his attitude of mind

William James

A study carried out by Harvard University found that 85 per cent of the reasons why people obtained job positions and succeeded in them was due to attitude and only 15 per cent to aptitude or technical expertise. Yet our Western education system spends 90 per cent of allocated funds on acquiring facts and figures and only 10 per cent on the development of attitudes necessary for success in later life. If we combine these two statistics, we find that we are spending 90 per cent of our educational time and money on developing that part of the individual responsible for only 15 per cent of their success and 10 per cent of our educational time and money on developing those qualities responsible for 85 per cent of their success.

Attitude defined

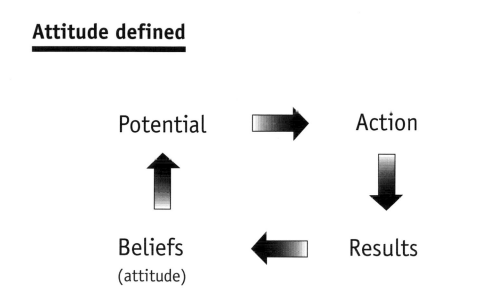

Figure 6: Attitude and results

If attitude is so important to success, what exactly is it? It is the most outwardly visible characteristic of what you think. It reflects the beliefs you hold and determines how you feel and behave. Your attitude is the result of the thoughts that you continually harbour. It's the cause and effect law in operation, thoughts being the cause and attitudes the effects. Norman Vincent Peale in his classic: *The Power of Positive Thinking* defined positive thinking as: 'A form of thought which **habitually** looks for the best out of the worst possible circumstances.' So your attitude, in effect, is your habit of thinking which, of course, is within your control and can, consequently, be changed if need be.

Your attitude reflects the beliefs you hold and determines how you feel and behave

Key Learning Point

There are many misconceptions about positive thinking. Many believe that positive thinkers walk around with their heads in the sand, ostrich-like, ignoring the realities of life. That is not true. Positive thinkers simply choose not to dwell on the negatives. They are aware of negative situations and take action when these arise.

Key Learning Point

Thinking, attitude, action and reaction

You know of people whose lives are pretty comfortable. They may even be considered successful achievers by others, yet, because perhaps 10 per cent of their life is not as they would like it to be, they choose to focus on that and ignore the 90 per cent that is working well. You will always receive from life what you choose to focus upon and therefore continually focusing on what you do not want will ensure you have more of it. So the positive thinkers choose to dwell on the positive aspects of their lives but when obstacles arise they treat these as negative feedback and look for positive solutions to them. Let's be clear about one thing. Positive *thinking* is not the panacea to all our ills. It is not an end in itself. On its own it will not change anything. Improved results come about through positive *action* which in turn depends on a positive mental *attitude*. And the prerequisite for a positive mental attitude is, of course, positive thinking.

Key Learning Point

Someone once said: 'Life comprises 10 per cent of what happens to us and 90 per cent of how we react to what happens to us.' Our reactions are determined by the attitudes that we hold. Consequently, if we wish to be a successful achiever we need to develop positive attitudes in order to react positively to situations.

'Life comprises 10 per cent of what happens to us and 90 per cent of how we react to what happens to us'

Often when we are feeling depressed or down for whatever reason we look outside of ourselves for the cause. More often than not if we examine our own attitudes and decide to change them, our mood changes accordingly. Let me illustrate this point by way of an example. A man was preparing a presentation for his company the next day but was having difficulty in finalising it and wanted a couple of hours of peace and quiet. However, his wife had just gone over to the neighbours for a cup of tea and his seven year old son was pestering him to such an extent that he could not concentrate on the report. Finally, in desperation, he tore a map of the world out of a magazine, ripped it into shreds and scattered the pieces over the lounge carpet. He then gave his son a tray and suggested to him that he piece together the map of the world as one would a jigsaw puzzle. He then retired to his study believing that he would have at least a couple of hours to concentrate on his report. However, this was not to be, as ten minutes later, in came his son and presented the tray to his father with the map of the world duly completed. His father was amazed at this and asked him how he had achieved it. His son responded by saying that on the other side of the map was a large photograph of a man and he figured if he got the man right the world would be right. Now there is a very simple message in that example. We cannot control everything that happens to us but we can control how we react to situations. In other words if we get ourselves right, our world will be right. And 'getting ourselves right' entails developing a positive mental attitude to life.

Practical steps to develop and sustain a positive mental attitude

Here then are some practical steps to develop and sustain a positive mental attitude:

Set goals

Firstly, you need to have written, challenging, specific, measurable and prioritised goals. These:

    a)   activate your subconscious mind;

    b)   re-energise your system;

    c)   alert you to the opportunities which may be around you all the time but, when goals are not written and imprinted on your subconscious mind, are largely ignored;

    d)   make your work a lot more fun.

Associate with achievers

We know that one of the quickest ways to catch influenza is to associate with people who have it. Well, the good news is that a positive mental attitude is equally as contagious and if you associate with positive minded people, it will have a direct bearing on your outlook and subsequent behaviour.

Develop a 'do your best' habit

You will greatly enhance your attitude if you develop a habit of doing your best in whatever situation you find yourself. It stands to reason that if you perform to the best of your ability in one particular activity and then adopt this same attitude the next time that same activity is performed, you will perform just a little better than previously and by continuing this process will grow and become more competent on a regular basis. Unfortunately, many people have the attitude of doing the minimum possible for the remuneration they receive. They are cheating themselves in the long run. All that this is doing is putting into your subconscious mind inferior performances repeatedly and that can only negatively condition you for subsequent results. By attempting to do your best in every situation and doing more than is expected of you in your particular job, you will grow and rise to the top of your vocation much more quickly than your contemporaries.

To enhance your attitude develop the habit of doing your best in whatever situation you find yourself

Key Learning Point

Enthusiasm

A necessary ingredient for a positive mental attitude is enthusiasm and this is, like other habits, developed through repetition of conscious acts. There are a number of ways to develop enthusiasm. The most obvious is to start acting enthusiastically in whatever you are doing. You will know that actors who are playing a role for a number of months tend to take on the characteristics and traits of the role they are playing. Similarly, you can begin acting enthusiastically in all your activities and you will soon find that you have adopted the trait as part of you. Another way to develop enthusiasm is to increase your interest in what you are doing. This is best accomplished by improving your knowledge and spending half an hour every day reading about your particular job or work situation. In this manner the acquisition of knowledge will lead to greater interest and, once again, this will assist you in rising above the average worker. You will also find by animating yourself – in other words by putting more into your work – that you develop a more enthusiastic approach to what you are doing. You can also choose to be an optimist rather than a pessimist as this will raise your enthusiasm level. It's like the old story of looking at half a glass of water. The optimist will say it's half full. The pessimist will say it's half empty. The reason is simple. The optimist is putting water in – the pessimist is taking water out. It's exactly the same in life – the optimist looks at what he can put into life whereas the pessimist is looking for what he can take from life.

Look for the positive side of people

Make it a habit to continually look for the positive traits in other people. Pay compliments wherever you can. Be the first to smile at other people and you will be amazed at the results that you get. (Obviously, walking around with a permanent grin on your face will have different results!)

See something positive in every situation

If you look for something positive in all situations, no matter how bleak they may appear to be at the outset, you will generally find them. By keeping your mind on what you want and off what you don't want, you will start to become solution rather than problem orientated and will look at possible alternatives whenever obstacles arise. You may recall the ex-heavyweight boxing champion of the world, Rocky Marciano who was undefeated after 49 defences of his title. When he first started his boxing career, he was advised by well-meaning boxing experts to give up the game. He was becoming virtually a punch bag for his opponents after the third or fourth round, as he was weak in his upper body and unable to keep his arms up in defence after the first few rounds. He also had very little power in his shoulders. Now most people receiving advice from these experts would have thought twice about continuing with their careers. However, Rocky Marciano had a burning desire to be a boxing champion and took this advice seriously but decided to turn his weaknesses into strengths. As a result, he undertook a lot of his training in a swimming pool and would take deep breaths and then submerge himself under the water where he would punch away using the resistance of the water to build up his shoulders and upper arms. Not only did he become much stronger in that department, but he also considerably improved his stamina because of his increase in lung capacity. His opponents later said that his greatest asset was his ability to relentlessly attack from the beginning to the end of the fight. In other words he had transformed a previous weakness into a strength. He saw something positive in what was apparently a very negative situation.

See something positive in every situation

Guide to Best Practice

Self belief

If you wish to develop a positive mental attitude you need to have belief in yourself. Having set yourself high goals you must now cultivate the belief that you are worthy of those goals by continually reminding yourself of your positive qualities and abilities to achieve. Regular reflection, at least weekly to begin with, of your personal achievements will help solidify this belief.

Record ideas immediately

When you have a positive mental attitude you will react to situations immediately and positively. This presupposes that you will be in a position to act on ideas that spring to mind immediately. For this, develop the habit of having a pencil or pen and paper with you at all times as, once you have embarked on a goal setting programme and are regularly conditioning yourself to achieve your goals, you will receive numerous ideas on how to reach them. You need to record them so that you can subsequently take action on them.

Success expectancy

Develop a success expectancy. This is a common characteristic of self-motivated winners as described in Chapter 6. When you cultivate the belief that you are a successful achiever and start attaining successes, no matter how small, you are developing the success habit and the expectancy of future successes will be far easier to maintain. Henry Ford was a good example of someone who expected success and achieved it. He asked his technicians to come up with a V8 engine. They told him after six months work that it could not be done. But he did not accept this. He believed that it could be done and that they were the best people available to design this engine. Another six months passed and they again told him that it was not possible to achieve. He again sent them back to the drawing boards reassuring them of his confidence in their ability to come up with the answer. Sure enough, six months later, the V8 engine was produced. This was purely because Henry Ford had a success expectancy. (You will find this works very well with your children. Expect them to succeed at what they are attempting and they will, more often than not, rise to those expectations.)

Count your blessings

A big inhibitor to developing a positive mental attitude is the widely held tendency to focus on weaknesses or mistakes and interpret them as obstacles to future progress. If you can see these as the inevitable stepping stones to success, they will be placed in their correct perspective. At times such as these, it pays to concentrate and remind yourself of your strengths. In other words: 'Count your blessings.' You will always find that you will have far more going for you than you ever have against you if you are objective and honest about your own qualities.

Positive emotions

You should also realise that there is a predominance of negativity around and that you will be in an environment where you will be bombarded with the opinions of other people which will largely be negative. You need to keep your own positive emotions charged and refuse to accept the opinions of people who tell you things cannot be done.

Obstacles

And finally, in developing a positive mental attitude you need to see the obstacles that you will inevitably encounter on your path to your goals as the challenges which they are. No successful person in this world ever achieved their own success without 'failing' first. However, their attitude towards that 'failure' was the determinant in their eventual success. They regarded it as a learning experience. Babe Ruth held the record for the greatest number of home runs in American baseball history at the same time as the record for the greatest number of strike-outs! Is he remembered for his successes or his 'failures'? So you should welcome your challenges when they arise as they give you an opportunity to use your initiative and creativity to overcome them and consequently to grow and use more of your potential.

Your attitude to life determines life's attitude to you

Key Learning Point

Your attitude towards life will invariably determine life's attitude towards you. Your success in life will depend upon your positive actions and these must be preceded by a positive mental attitude which can only be cultivated by consistent positive thinking. Remember that your mind is like a garden. In a garden if you planted bean seeds, you would not expect potatoes to grow. In the same way you cannot expect positive results if you have planted negative seeds. So you must take charge of that conditioning process. Start sewing positive seeds daily.

Summary

1. Attitude is the most outwardly visible characteristic of what you think. It reflects the beliefs you hold and determines how you feel and behave.

2. Positive thinkers choose not to dwell on negatives but when negative situations arise take positive action to resolve them.

3. You will always receive from life what you choose to focus upon and by continually focusing upon what you do not want will ensure you have more of it. The positive thinker chooses to focus on the part of his life that is working well.

4. Positive thinking is not the panacea to all our ills. It is not an end in itself. It is a vital link in the chain involving thinking, beliefs, expectations, attitudes, feelings, behaviours and results.

5. Life comprises 10 per cent of what happens to us and 90 per cent of how we react to what happens to us. Our reactions are determined by the attitudes that we hold.

6. Practical steps to develop and sustain a positive mental attitude are:

    a) Set written, challenging, specific, measurable and prioritised goals.

    b) Associate with achievers.

    c) Cultivate a 'do your best' habit.

    d) Develop enthusiasm.

    e) Look for the positive side of people.

    f) Believe in yourself.

    g) Record ideas immediately.

    h) Expect success.

    i) Count your blessings.

     j)   Keep your own positive emotions charged.

     k)   See obstacles as the challenges that they are.

7.   Your attitude towards life will determine life's attitude towards you. By putting more into life you will receive more from it. But it must start with GIVING.

If this is your first reading of this book, please proceed to Chapter 9. If this is your second or subsequent reading, please carry out Activities 35, 36, 37, 38, 39, 40 and 41.

Activity No. 35

Attitude questionnaire

Answer the following questions as quickly and honestly as you can. The first answer that comes to mind is usually the most accurate.

No.	QUESTION	Yes – Always	Some-times	No – Never
1.	Do you write down specific goals and plans for attainment within the next five years?			
2.	Can you control your own attitude in any situation?			
3.	When things go wrong, do you tend to look at what you can learn from the setback to help your future actions?			
4.	Do you pay compliments to people?			
5.	Are you able to keep your mind on what you want and off what you do not want?			
6.	Would your friends and colleagues describe you as 'an enthusiastic optimist '?			
7.	Do you look upon rejections or 'failures' as the natural 'stepping stones' to success?			
8.	Do you act on your ideas as soon as they come to mind?			

No.	QUESTION	Yes – Always	Some-times	No – Never
9.	Do you frequently remind yourself of your past successes?			
10.	Do you actively focus on controlling your attitude to influence your feelings and behaviour?			
11.	Do you record your life by means of a two-page-per-day diary or journal?			
12.	Are you the first to introduce yourself in social situations?			
13.	Do you expect successful outcomes from your actions?			
14.	Are you able to positively influence the mood of the group you are in?			
15.	Do you tend to focus on what is going right with your life instead of what is not going right?			
16.	Do you associate with enthusiastic goal directed achievers?			
17.	Do you look at the possible benefits of changes rather than the limitations?			
18.	When changes lead to stress are you able to control your reactions?			

No.	QUESTION	Yes – Always	Some-times	No – Never
19.	Do you take regular physical exercise to maintain your health and energy level?			
20.	Do you eat high-water content foods?			
21.	Do you regularly engage in some form of autogenic conditioning, meditation, or other creative visualisation technique?			
22.	Do you help others to achieve their goals?			
23.	Do you make decisions quickly and change them rarely?			
24.	Are others in the habit of coming to you for advice?			
25.	Can you lift yourself out of a depressed state by controlling your physiology and mental focus?			

Scoring

Score: 4 points for every YES – ALWAYS

2 points for every SOMETIMES

0 points for every NO – NEVER

Evaluation

If you have scored between:

80 – 100   **Excellent** – you have the right mental attitude to become one of life's 'winners' if you are not already one.

60 – 80   **Above average** – your overall attitude is good and coupled with the application of proven success principles, should ensure the attainment of your goals in life.

40 – 60   **Average** – if you are serious about using your true potential and consistently achieving results in life, your attitude will have to improve.

Below 40   **Poor** – your first decision should be to work on your attitude as, unless you do so, your chances of achieving success commensurate with your potential are minimal.

Activity

Activity No. 36

Identifying positive thinking goal achievers

Make a list below of the people who you consider to be positive thinking, goal orientated achievers and with whom you would wish to associate on a regular basis. Plan to contact at least two of them during the next week to discuss your goals and plans with them. (Diarise this *now*!) Record the outcome of your meetings.

Goal orientated achievers with a positive mental attitude with whom I would like to meet regularly

_____

_____

_____

Outcome of meeting No. 1

Outcome of meeting No. 2

Activity No. 37

Identifying positive and negative associations

Select a situation, such as a job or a relationship, which plays an important part in your life. Write down all the positive things you can think of in connection with it, and all the negative associations. Now compare the two lists. What do they tell you?

Description of situation	
Positives	**Negatives**

If your negative associations outweigh the positives, you need to change your attitude or your situation. Always start with yourself. Try looking at all possible positive outcomes. Remember – you have complete control over your attitude – if you choose to exercise it. Now carry out Activity No. 38.

Activity

Activity No. 38

Obtaining positive outcomes from negative situations/people

During the course of the next week, write down every negative situation that arises. Then write down what possible positive outcomes could emerge from them. Similarly, with people. If you encounter negative people, look for some positive qualities in their make-up. If you search, you will find.

Negative situation or person	Possible positive outcome or qualities

Activity

Activity No. 39

Cultivating a 'best' attitude

Select certain activities associated with your major goals in both your work and personal situations. The next time you perform those activities make sure you 'give them your best shot'. Record the outcome. Try to choose activities the results of which can be measured. Follow this same procedure for the whole week and then compare your results at the end of that week. There should be a marked improvement in measured outcomes as you progressively repeat the activities.

Description of activity	Outcome (measurable where possible)
A	1
Repeat of activity A	2
Repeat of activity A	3
Repeat of activity A	4
B	1
Repeat of activity B	2
Repeat of activity B	3
Repeat of activity B	4
C	1
Repeat of activity C	2
Repeat of activity C	3
Repeat of activity C	4

Description of activity	Outcome (measurable where possible)
D	1
Repeat of activity D	2
Repeat of activity D	3
Repeat of activity D	4
E	1
Repeat of activity E	2
Repeat of activity E	3
Repeat of activity E	4

Activity

Activity No. 40

Reminder of past week's successes

You should, by now, be using a two page-per-day diary regularly or the 'To Do' list as outlined in Activity No. 18. Set aside at least an hour over the weekend to reflect on your successes of the past week. Go through all the scheduled activities and appointments and re-call your feelings when the activities were successfully completed or your meetings resulted in positive outcomes for you and your company *(see opposite)*.

Successes over past week	Feelings on successful completion

Activity No. 41

Daily attitude shaping questions

Every morning, immediately following your autogenic conditioning session, ask yourself the following questions to shape your attitude for the day.

1. What is great about my life right now?

2. What areas of my life are really satisfying?

3. Who can I compliment or praise today?

4. How can I give of myself to help others today?

5. Which person or organisation can I help today?

6. How best can I express my love for my (wife, husband, son, daughter, father, mother, boyfriend, girlfriend, etc) today?

7. What am I committed to accomplishing today?

Your personal
health programme

Chapter 9

Nutritional awareness

A sensible diet coupled with a regular exercise programme is the best formula for maintaining good health. Every individual is unique and requires analysis of his or her own nutritional needs based on variables such as their environment, their height, weight, medical condition and so on. Consequently, before embarking on any new dietary regimen you should consult a nutritionist.

If you either eat the wrong food stuffs or the incorrect combinations of the right food stuffs, you over-burden your digestive system. Digestion of your food consumes more energy than heavy aerobic activity. In fact, digestion is the greatest single drain on your energy level. By eating the right foods and by ensuring that you avoid combining carbohydrates and proteins in the same meal, you are conserving your energy for activities other than digestion.

There is so much controversy these days about what we should and should not be putting into our bodies that, understandably, people become confused. This tends to reinforce the natural reluctance to change existing eating habits. (In any event, most people could find some form of justification for their present consumption pattern, if they searched hard enough!) I strongly recommend that in developing your own personal health programme you consult a nutritionist to determine the right foods to consume to reach your health and fitness goals and which foods to avoid.

Your emotions have a direct influence on your physiology and consequently when you harbour feelings of anger, resentment, hatred, anxiety, doubt and so on these are like physical poisons to your system and weaken your immune system.

Most of the bugs that cause disease or illness reside within our bodies already and we should recognise that instead of trying to find ways of eradicating these entirely, we should be concentrating on strengthening our resistance to them. It is very much the same with life itself. It is never possible to remove all the obstacles in our path to our goals – and fortunately so. Without any obstacles there would be no sense of achievement. In the same way as we need a resistance of weights to build body muscles, so we need the challenges of these bugs within our system to build up our resistance towards them. They are inherently part of nature and we should learn to live in balance with them.

Physical fitness

A physical fitness programme coupled with a sensible diet is essential for optimising your health. The benefits of having a physical fitness programme are many. It will lower your blood pressure, decrease your resting heart rate, strengthen your muscles (including your heart), increase your blood vessels and improve the quality of your blood by intensifying the oxygen content. Before embarking on any physical fitness programme, you should consult your doctor and let him know what you intend to do in the form of physical exercise. Aerobic exercises are the best as they greatly increase the flow of oxygen and blood to all parts of the body. To be fully effective the exercise must raise the heart rate to a certain level and keep it at that level for not less than 10 to 15 minutes. Obviously, if you are not in condition, you will have to build up slowly to a 15 minute sustained period. Examples of aerobic activities are cycling, running, jogging, swimming, skipping and vigorous walking. Stop/start exercises like golf, cricket, show jumping, house-work, gardening and so on as well as those exercises which have a short duration such as sprinting, dancing and calisthenics are not truly effective in producing the desired level of fitness.

Aerobic exercises have many benefits, the most important of which are:

a) The conversion of fat to muscle leading to the more efficient utilisation of calories.

b) Increased energy and stamina.

c) Improved appearance – a more positive self image and outlook on life.

d) Improvement of general circulation through the strengthening of the heart, lungs and muscles. This usually has the added benefit of reducing blood pressure and slowing down the heart rate.

e) Reduction of nervous tension and depression.

f) More restful sleep.

g) Improved absorption and utilisation of food.

h) The body's natural tendency is then to consume far fewer drugs, caffeine, alcohol, tobacco, sugar and refined carbohydrates.

You should start your exercise programme gradually and then build up to 35 to 40 minutes of aerobic activities, four or five times a week. Remember that before starting any programme you should get your doctor's consent for what you intend to do.

To gain the maximum benefit from your exercise programme, you should neither over exert yourself nor do too little. The chart at the end of this section can be used as a guide to the heart rate at which you should exercise to achieve maximum benefits safely. Locate your age in the left hand column and follow it across to the second column to determine your recommended training pulse rate. If you have had any history of heart disease then go to the third column. In this latter case, it would be imperative for you to get your doctor's approval before commencing any exercise programme.

You will know if you are exercising too strenuously by one of the following indicators:

a) If you start feeling faint or become dizzy or nauseous, have any tightness or pain in your chest, shortness of breath or loss of muscle control – stop exercising immediately.

b) Take your pulse five minutes after exercise. It should have returned to 120 or below. If it has not, you are exercising too hard. Take your pulse again after ten minutes. It should now be below 100 beats per minute. If it is not then you need to ease up a little on your exercise programme.

c) If you find yourself short of breath ten minutes after exercising, then it is too strenuous.

d) Your exercise programme should be stimulating and invigorating. However, if you find yourself worn out and tired all the time, it is a sure sign that you are overdoing it and should ease up.

Regular aerobic exercise has tremendous value for your health, mainly due to the improvement in the quality of your blood cells through increased oxygenation and circulation. The most important element of cellular health is oxygen and correct breathing will greatly assist your regular aerobic exercises in maximising the oxygen supply to your blood cells as well as stimulating the lymphatic system which eliminates toxins from the body. In fact there is nothing that creates greater stimulation of the lymphatic system than deep diaphragmatic breathing.

Unfortunately, most people are unaware of the benefits of deep abdominal breathing. When you breathe properly, the diaphragm contracts and the abdomen protrudes allowing the lungs to expand and fill with air. So I would suggest you take notice of how you breathe normally and if you find that you tend to take quick shallow breaths from the chest, change this deliberately and make a point three times a day of taking ten very deep breaths in for say five seconds and then exhaling for ten seconds each time. If you develop the habit of doing this exercise of ten deep breaths three times a day for a month, you will notice tremendous differences in your energy level and your overall state of vitality.

Heart rates (based on a resting heart rate of 72 for male and 80 for female)

Age	Recommended training pulse rate	Heart disease history (not to exceed)
20	160	150
22	158	148
24	157	147
25	155	145
28	154	144
30	152	143
32	151	142
34	150	140
36	149	140
38	147	138
40	146	137
45	143	134
50	140	131
55	137	128
60	128	120
65	120	113

Note: If your resting pulse rate is more than 12 beats per minute slower, determine your recommended training rate from this formula: Your recommended training rate equals .65 x (recommended training rate in the table minus your resting rate) plus your resting rate. (The value you compute from this formula should be less than the value in the table.)

Example

A man of 50 has a resting heart/pulse rate of 55. His recommended training rate is:

0,65 x (140 − 55) + 55 = 110

Stress management

These days, with the hectic pace that people are expected to maintain, stress has become an increasingly contributing factor to poor health. Of course, a certain amount of stress is beneficial for achieving results. However, when that stress becomes excessive, it tends to find the weakest link in our system and certainly has psychologically damaging effects such as depression, irritability, insomnia, heart disease, ulcers, headaches, lethargy and so on.

Stress symptoms

There are many symptoms of stress – high blood pressure, dizziness, palpitations, sweaty palms, cold hands or feet, rapid heart beat, sudden bursts of energy, migraine headaches, chest pains, shortness of breath, a change in appetite, nausea, gas pains or cramps, acid stomach, heartburn, problems with urination, constipation, diarrhoea, frigidity or impotence, dry mouth or throat, muscular pains, tension headaches, trembling or shaking.

Avoiding stressors

Here are some practical ways to avoid the effects of stress which should be built into your own personal health programme. Firstly, again concentrating on prevention rather than cure, try to avoid known stressors such as interruptions, noisy neighbours, poorly lighted offices, overcrowding, job overload, rush-hour traffic, strict deadlines, rigid bureaucracy and irritating people. Secondly, you can alter your body's response to stressful situations seeing as it is not always possible to avoid the stressors outlined above. Your body's response can be altered both indirectly by changing your mental set and emotional habits and directly by tuning up your body's physical system by exercise and meditation.

Where stress is concerned, prevention is always better than cure

Stress control

Stress can best be controlled by:

a) Ensuring at least seven to eight hours of sleep every night.

b) Having a nutritional breakfast.

c) Having three adequate meals a day with no snacks in between them.

d) Exercising at least four times a week for a minimum of 35 minutes per session. (Consult your doctor before commencing any vigorous exercise programme.)

e) Restricting alcohol intake to one or two drinks per day.

f) Maintaining a normal relationship between your height and your weight. (Consult your doctor if in any doubt.)

g) Not smoking.

h) Restricting your intake of tea, coffee or soft drinks containing caffeine to two or three cups per day at most.

i)   Scheduling regular periods of meditation. If you are now carrying out your creative visualisation sessions (autogenic conditioning) for 20 minutes twice a day, this will be sufficient.

j)   Enjoying your life and making sure that you take breaks frequently. In this regard, try to take at least two weeks holiday every year.

Summary

Key Learning Point

To summarise, a personal health programme is really a matter of common sense. I have stressed in this chapter the need to consult with your doctor before commencing an exercise programme and embarking on a new diet. If you are to maximise your potential and achieve personal success in your life then being healthy forms an integral part of that process. You will become healthy if you follow certain basic health habits such as:

a)   Develop the habit of deep diaphragmatic breathing.

b)   Regular aerobic exercise (at least 35 to 40 minutes four to five times per week).

c)   Your diet should comprise 70 per cent or more high water content foods (fruit, vegetables, salads and sprouts).

d)   Recommended diet:

i)   Ensure correct food combinations. Do not eat protein and carbohydrates at the same meal.

ii) Breakfast: Fruit and fruit juices (fresh not processed) until noon. Quantity dictated by your hunger and thirst levels.

iii) Lunch: Large salad – high water content ingredients.

iv) Dinner: Lots of vegetables (steamed) with either protein or carbohydrates – not both.

e)   Your mind greatly influences your physiology. Ensure that your mind is constantly directed towards positive outcomes. Carry out autogenic conditioning twice a day, 20 minutes each session.

f)   Ensure you have sufficient rest to build up your energy, sunshine to improve your metabolism (without overdoing exposure), and muscular relaxation or massage.

g)   Minimise or preferably avoid entirely: fats, animal flesh, dairy products, sugar, salt, vinegar, tobacco, alcohol, coffee and other caffeine containing beverages, and drugs (both prescription and over-the-counter).

If this is your first reading of this book, please proceed to Chapter 10. If this is your second or subsequent reading, please carry out Activities 42 to 45.

Activity

Activity No. 42

Effective breathing exercise

To improve the effectiveness of your lymphatic system as well as to increase your energy levels, deep diaphragmatic breathing should be carried out three times a day, each session consisting of ten deep breathing cycles involving inhalation for a certain number of seconds followed by exhalation for twice the inhalation period.

Stand with your feet shoulder width apart and raise your arms parallel to the floor. Bend your elbows so that your hands are almost touching your chest and the fingertips facing each other but just apart. Now, using two movements, firstly, keeping your arms bent at the elbow, pull your arms back as far as they will go before returning them to the starting position. Secondly, straighten your arms so that they are fully outstretched and virtually become extensions of your shoulders with your right arm pointing to your right and your left arm pointing to your left (the cross position) before again returning them to the starting position. Now breathe in deeply through the nose and count the number of completed movements it takes you to completely fill your lungs, before exhaling over twice the number of completed movements. Do this ten times every morning, noon and evening for a month and notice how much more energy and vitality you then have.

The Holmes-Rahe scale (stress rating indicator guide)

This stress rating scale was first published as early as 1967 by Doctors T.H. Holmes and R.H. Rahe of the University of Washington Medical School, and has been in constant use since then because of its extremely high (80 per cent+) predictability record concerning the chances of falling ill or contracting some disease.

Go through each of the 43 life events listed. For those events that have taken place in your life over the past 12 months enter the appropriate 'Mean Value' in the adjacent 'Your Score' column. Then add up all of your scores (both pages) to reach a total.

If you have scored 150 or less, you are considered to be free of the risk of disease due to stress related factors.

If you have scored between 150 or 300, you are considered to be suffering from moderate stress due to your life changes and, consequently, have a 50-50 chance of becoming ill or disabled within the next two years.

If you have scored 300 or more, you are considered to be suffering from heavy stress due to your life changes and, consequently, you have reached a critical plateau in your life and have a high probability (in excess of 50 per cent) of becoming seriously ill within the next year.

Depending on your score, you may wish to adopt certain lifestyle changes to cope more effectively with your stressors, such as autogenic conditioning, meditation, deep (power) breathing, proper nutrition (high water content diet) and regular physical exercise (see Activity No. 44).

The Holmes-Rahe scale

Life event	Mean value	Your score
Death of spouse	100	
Divorce	73	
Marital separation	65	
Jail term	63	
Death of close family member	63	
Personal injury or illness	53	
Marriage	50	
Fired at work	47	
Marital reconciliation	45	
Retirement	45	
Change in health of family member	44	
Pregnancy	40	
Sex difficulties	39	
Gain of new family member	39	
Business adjustment	39	
Change in financial status	38	
Death of close friend	37	
Change to different line of work	36	
Increase in number of arguments with spouse	35	
New mortgage	31	
Foreclosure of mortgage or loan	30	
Change in responsibilities at work	29	
Son or daughter leaving home	29	
Trouble with in-laws	29	
	TOTAL C/F	

Life event	Mean value	Your score
	Total B/F	
Outstanding personal achievement	28	
Spouse begins or stops work	26	
Child begins or ends school	26	
Change in living conditions	25	
Revision of personal habits	24	
Trouble with boss	23	
Change in work hours or conditions	20	
Change in residence	20	
Change in schools	20	
Change in recreation	19	
Change in church activities	19	
Change in social activities	18	
Loan less than £50,000.00	17	
Change in sleeping habits	16	
Change in number of family get–togethers	15	
Change in eating habits	15	
Vacation	13	
Christmas	12	
Minor violations of the law	11	
	TOTAL	

Source : Adapted from Thomas H. Holmes and Richard H. Rahe, *Social Readjustment Rating Scale*, 1967.

Activity No. 44

Stress management programme

If you scored above 150 on the Holmes-Rahe Scale in Activity No. 43, you should take immediate steps to implement a stress management programme. Using the programme outlined below as a general guide, consult your doctor and nutritionist to discuss the 'tailoring' or 'fine tuning' of the programme to meet your specific needs.

1. Ensure adequate sleep (seven to eight hours every night).

2. Maintain a nutritional diet:

    a – Breakfast, fruit and fruit juice (natural, not processed).

    b – Lunch, salad (high water content).

    c – Dinner, steam-cooked vegetables with either protein or carbohydrate – not both.

3. Minimise snacks between meals. If you must eat something then try fresh or sun-dried fruit.

4. Exercise aerobically at least four times a week for a minimum of 35 minutes per session.

5. Carry out autogenic conditioning twice a day for 20 minutes per session.

6. Do not smoke.

7. Restrict your intake of alcohol to one or two drinks per day. Better still abstain altogether!

8. Restrict your intake of coffee, tea or soft drinks containing caffeine to two or three cups/glasses per day at most. Again, if you can do without any caffeine beverage at all (replace with fresh fruit juice or filtered/mineral water), so much the better for your stress resilience.

9. Regularly carry out power breathing exercises. (See Activity No. 42).

10. Take frequent breaks and try to go on at least a two week vacation every year.

Activity No. 45

Your personal exercise and dietary programme

Set yourself a physical fitness goal and a deadline for its attainment. Now decide on the physical activities that you will enjoy performing as well as the nutritional diet that you intend adhering to, to help you reach your goal.

You should now consult your doctor and your nutritionist to discuss your present and desired physical condition and your proposed programme for achieving it. Based on their feedback and advice, modify your programme accordingly and enter your revised programme onto the next page. (If necessary, go back to Activity No.9 and update your plan.)

Transfer your planned activities to your diary or 'To Do' list.

1.   Physical fitness goal:

_____

_____ Deadline: _____

2.   Physical activities/sports/exercises to be performed to attain the goal:

Activity   Duration/session   Sessions/week

_____

_____

_____

_____

3. Diet:

   a) Breakfast options: _____

   _____

   b) Lunch options: _____

   _____

   c) Dinner options: _____

   _____

   d) Snacks options: _____

   _____

   e) Vitamin or mineral supplements: _____

   _____

Conclusion

I mentioned in the introduction to this book that as far as personal success is concerned there are literally millions of people who know what to do and how to do it but never get around to actually doing it. While their inspiration may be high and their interest well-developed, they have not programmed themselves with new behavioural habits. They will therefore continue doing what they have always done but strangely enough, expect different results! This is ludicrous as there is no chance of these expectations being realised. If your present behaviour is not producing the results you truly desire, you must change it. Hence the need to re-programme yourself for success. The acquisition of new behavioural habits involves the conscious repetition of certain activities for a period of time (usually between 21 and 30 days) until they become subconsciously automatic.

Daily rituals

To develop your own personal success habits, I recommend that you repeat the following 'rituals' daily for a consecutive period of 30 days:

1. Carry with you at all times your 3" x 5" goal affirmation cards relating to your four major goals and empowering beliefs and read them aloud to yourself at least three times a day (in addition to the two readings during your autogenic conditioning sessions).

2. Twice a day, preferably first thing in the morning after waking up and last thing before returning at night, carry out autogenic conditioning for 20 minutes a session (Activity 1).

3. Ask yourself the Daily Attitude Shaping Questions (Activity 41).

4. Have your goals poster where you will see it at least twice a day (Activity 11).

5. Rewrite your four major goal statements and plans daily for 30 consecutive days (Activities 10 and 28). After about two weeks you

should have much greater clarity over your goals and plans. You can now construct mind maps of each plan and refer to them daily when compiling your 'To Do' lists.

6. Ensure that you compile your daily 'To Do' list with no more than six important items you intend accomplishing that day in priority order and with a time allocated for their completion.

7. You then need to obtain feedback on your progress towards your goals and how you have performed regarding your prioritised activities. This can best be done by using a two-page-per-day diary and recording the events and happenings of each day as they arise. Consequently, whatever action you take in pursuance of your goals, the results of those actions can be recorded on the opposite page. If you do not have a two-page-per-day diary then I suggest you start a journal (Activity 18).

8. Take corrective action based on the feedback received. This entails replanning but should never result in the lowering of your goals.

9. Practice triggering your most resourceful state in daily situations (Activity 30).

10. Health:

    *   Breathing: 10 power breaths, three times daily (see Activity 42)

    *   Exercise: 35 – 40 minutes of aerobic activity, 4 – 5 times a week (see Activity 45)

    *   Diet: Fresh fruit/fruit juice up to noon. Salad for lunch (high water content). Vegetables (raw or steamed) with either protein or carbohydrate for dinner – NOT both. Try to minimise your intake of sugar, salt, caffeine, vinegar, dairy products, animals fats, tobacco and alcohol (see Activity 45).

Key Learning Point

A book released a few years ago entitled: *In the Mind's Eye*, and published by the National Research Council of America, investigated a variety of personal development programmes to determine their long-term effectiveness. The results were rather interesting. They found that human performance could best be enhanced by the synergistic effect of combining different processes. Whilst improvements could be gained through employing individual techniques, they had limited long-term effects. A variety of self improvement methods were investigated ranging from psychotherapy, Eastern religions, meditation, metaphysics, hypnotism, mysticism, spiritualism, creative thinking, Neuro-Linguistic Programming, bio-feedback techniques, auto-suggestion, light-sound synchronisation, use of subliminal cassette tapes, alpha mind training, hypno-peripheral process tapes, Gestalt therapy, behaviour modification, experiential learning and group training methods such as the Delphi technique, amongst others.

The research found that in addition to the effectiveness of the combination of these individual processes, long-term retention was enhanced when the learner was an active participant rather than a passive observer in the training process. In other words, when a 'learning by doing' philosophy was employed and participants had the opportunity of applying the principles learnt on the programme to their own individual situations, the results of the programme had much greater longevity. The results were even more long lasting when refresher training and follow-up mechanisms were provided. You have been supplied with a wide selection of techniques and methods for personal success in this book and are now in a position to learn them by carrying out the activities. Your progress, and it can be phenomenal progress, depends entirely on the extent of your application.

The power of choice

Many years ago I had the good fortune to interview, for television, the most widely read, self-help and inspirational author in the world – Og Mandino. When asked what he believed was our greatest power, he responded: 'The freedom of choice. Every day we exercise choice in the decisions we make. For instance, you decided to wear those clothes today and to be here at this time to interview me. In exactly the same way, we can choose to be successful.' The follow-up question was: 'Do people readily accept this – are they aware of this power to **choose** success?' He replied: 'No – that is the problem. People do not, as a rule, believe that they have what it takes to get to wherever they choose to go, probably because of previous conditioning which can be changed by regular self affirmations.' When questioned about on-going drive, he believed that sustaining motivation boils down to eliminating bad habits and that this was best achieved by replacing them with good ones through regular conditioning. Og Mandino added that the reason most people do not realise their true potential is not because of their inability to succeed or, for that matter, the lack of knowledge of what to do and how to do it; it is rather the lack of application – they do not discipline themselves to do what they know they should do. This, in turn, implies that there is insufficient desire.

'Our greatest power is our freedom of choice'   Og Mandino

Key Learning Point

Once you have acquired the habit of personal success, it doesn't necessarily follow that you will not slip back into previous negative habit patterns. This will depend very much on the strength of your previous negative habits and the degree to which you have conditioned your new ones. If you do find yourself slipping, then do what most of the successful people do in this situation. They simply tell themselves to go back to basics. Gary Player, one of the greatest golfers of all time, is never above asking other golfers what he may be doing wrong in their eyes if his game is not 'on song'. Now nobody would presume to tell Gary Player how he should hold the club, stand, swing, hold his head etc. Yet these are the very questions Gary asks of other golfers so that he can get back to basics and build from there. It is certainly a formula that has stood him in good stead throughout the years. He is still winning tournaments on the seniors circuit to this day!

So if you catch yourself falling back into old negative habit patterns, ask yourself whether you are still carrying out your daily rituals, particularly the autogenic conditioning sessions for 20 minutes twice a day. That should be the last exercise you ever sacrifice in your day. It is absolutely vital for you to maintain your desire at a high level so as to give you the drive to carry out your plans of action. Regular autogenic conditioning is the fastest and most effective way to re-kindle and sustain desire. In this way, you will be able to adopt the relevant principles for lasting change, instill the empowering beliefs that you need to attain your goals, control your emotions so that they work for rather than against you, and develop a consistently positive attitude towards life.

Key Learning Point

Regular autogenic conditioning is the fastest and most effective way to sustain desire

In any endeavour, it is a fact that the more tense you are, the less likely you are to succeed. The corollary applies in that the more relaxed you are at the start of any undertaking, the greater your chances of success. You can rid yourself of inhibiting tension and develop a far more relaxed yet effective approach to your daily activities again through the use of regular autogenic conditioning.

If I seem to be over emphasising the value of autogenic conditioning, believe me I am not. It is by far the best way to get in touch with your inner resources. I have no doubt in my own mind that this is a means of tuning into Infinite Intelligence, the Universal Mind, – your 'God' power within you. Once you start developing your higher self through the use of that power, and use it to help other people, your personal success is guaranteed.

One of the world's top insurance companies, many of whose consultants have participated in our personal development programmes, have a three-rule formula for success in the insurance business:

Rule 1.   See the people.

Rule 2.   See the people.

Rule 3.   See the people.

In other words, the insurance consultants' goal every day should be to 'see the people'. When those consultants come onto our programme, we explain that there is always a cause and effect relationship between an action plan and its intended goal. If the intended goal is to 'see the people', the plan must be to telephone for appointments. That is the initial cause and is what we encourage participants on the programmes to list as their daily 'must' activity. When they arrive at the office in the morning they know that their immediate goal that day is to make, for example, 20 telephone calls and they may set aside two hours of their time to achieve this. Their goal, the effect, may well be to make four to five appointments as a result of the 20 phone calls, the cause. However, their 'must' activity is the making of the calls rather than the securing of the appointments. It's a numbers game and once they have developed the habit of regularly making their 20 phone calls per day, they will gradually find that their ratio of the number of appointments to telephone calls made starts improving and thereafter, the goals of four or five appointments per day can be focused upon. What I am trying to get across here is that we need initially to concentrate upon the most important and immediate activity within our control, which in the example just outlined, is the making of appointments. 'Winning starts with beginning.' Once you have begun to build up momentum by carrying out your daily 'must' activities, you will soon acquire the success habit. It takes discipline to conscientiously follow your plan at the outset, particularly when you are receiving a lot of negative feed-back. The answer at this stage is to remember that what you are doing is very much based on numbers and that using the example on page 281, the more phone calls you make the more appointments you will eventually secure and thus the greater the number of sales you will obtain. You, therefore, need to view the telephone as your conduit to personal success. Mentally, you need to associate pleasure with picking up that phone and speaking to your potential customer.

Winning starts with beginning

Having read thus far, you now know what to do and how to do it. But, as I have stated on more than one occasion already, knowing what to do and how to do it is never enough. The answer to positive change and personal success lies in the action steps that you need to take. You also know by now that in order to take these action steps and produce results on a consistent basis, you need to have developed certain behavioural habits which are acquired through the daily programming of your conscious thoughts. The harsh reality is that nothing in your life will change without action and despite the best intentions in the world, that action will not materialise until you change the fundamental cause – your thinking. On our Personal Development Programmes which extend over a month, we are able to offer a full money-back guarantee on the results because we have the participants there long enough for them to acquire these new success habits and ensure that they are making measurable progress towards their goals by means of practical assignments.

At this point I want you to use your new-found powers of visualisation. I would like you to imagine me down on my knees pleading with you, begging you, imploring you to tackle the practical activities in this book – with absolute commitment to your own personal success. Set aside a time for yourself every day when you can work on these activities. Now I know that you intend to do them at some stage in the future. The world is full of people filled with good intentions which unfortunately very rarely materialise. I suggest you stop reading at this point and compile for yourself a time-table over the course of the next month when you will work through the activities at the end of each chapter. Then ask yourself this question every morning: 'What am I committed to doing today which will take me closer to one of my major goals?' Every evening ask yourself this question: 'What have I done today that has taken me closer to one of my major goals?' Ideally, the answers to both questions should be the same. However, we do not live in an ideal world and you know as well as I that situations are likely to arise which could disrupt your best laid plans. That should not deter you. In fact you should get used to that sort of thing happening. That is what life is all about. It is never what happens to you but rather how you react to what happens that determines your success.

Key Learning Point

Determining your success

You now have your own Personal Success System. You know how to use left and right brain hemispheres together. You know how to set your goals in the seven areas of your life and you have developed plans of how to get there. You have been given time management tips to employ to help you become a more effective and productive person. You have been shown how to improve your self-image and self-confidence as well as how to motivate yourself on a consistent basis and create an environment within which others can become self motivated. You know how to develop and sustain a positive mental attitude, to maintain maximum health and vitality and finally, you now know how to regularly programme yourself for the success that you desire. The theory is fine. The principles are all proven and will work for you as they have worked for thousands of others who have APPLIED them. I would suggest you read through the summaries at the end of each chapter and then get stuck into the activities.

Action Checklist

There is a simple six step formula for you to follow if you are serious about attaining personal success:

1. *Set written, challenging, specific, measurable, and prioritised goals.*

2. *Visualise the end results.*

3. *Plan your course of action.*

4. *Take action.*

5. *Obtain feed-back on the action steps taken.*

6. *Take corrective action where necessary.*

That formula, if followed, will lead you to inevitable success and once you have completed all the activities in this book and have consequently programmed yourself for success, you will be in a position to follow that formula.

It is now over to you. In the introduction to this book I asked you to make a commitment to yourself to take responsibility for your own destiny. Now that you have reached this point and know what to do and how to do it, I ask you to make the most important decision in your life – decide to apply the principles and techniques by carrying out the activities in this book. Only by doing that will you be mastering personal and interpersonal skills.

I wish you every success.